EYEWITNESS
HUMAN BODY

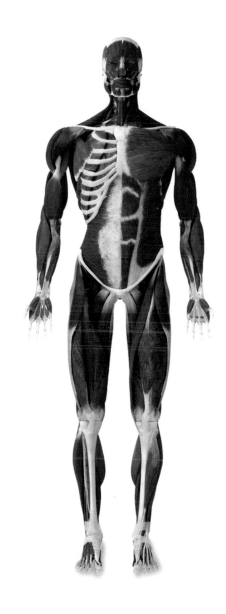

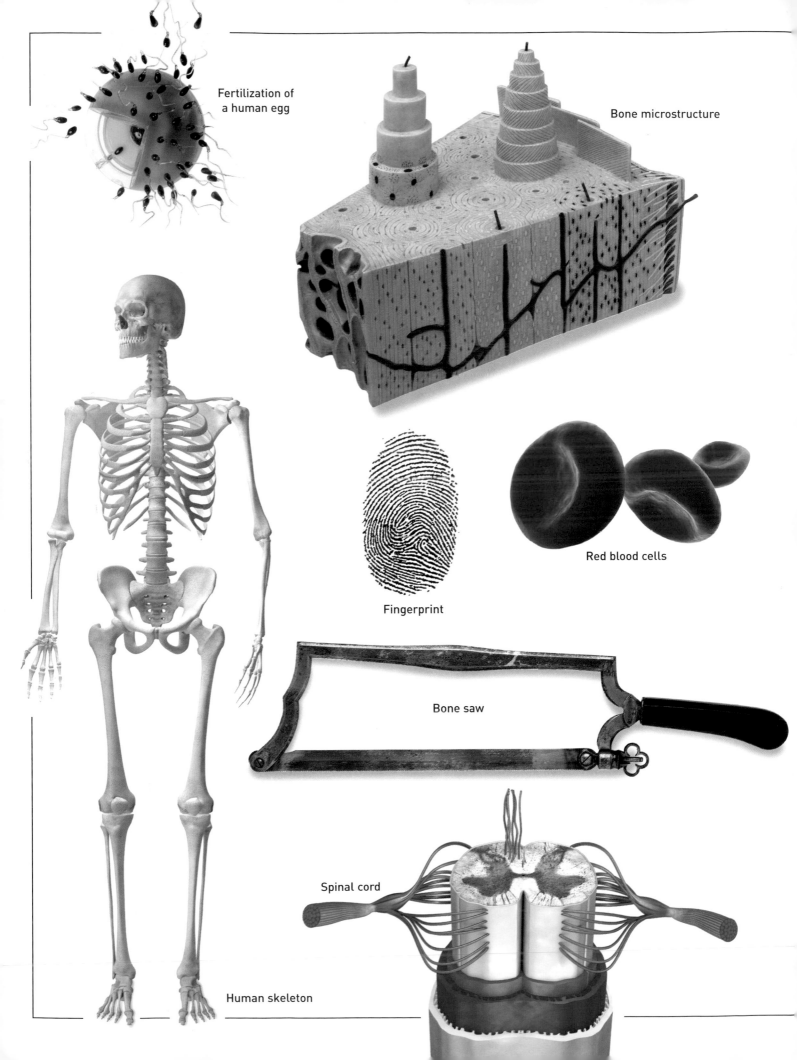

Fertilization of a human egg

Bone microstructure

Red blood cells

Fingerprint

Bone saw

Spinal cord

Human skeleton

Compound microscope

EYEWITNESS
HUMAN
BODY

Written by
Richard Walker

Nerve cell

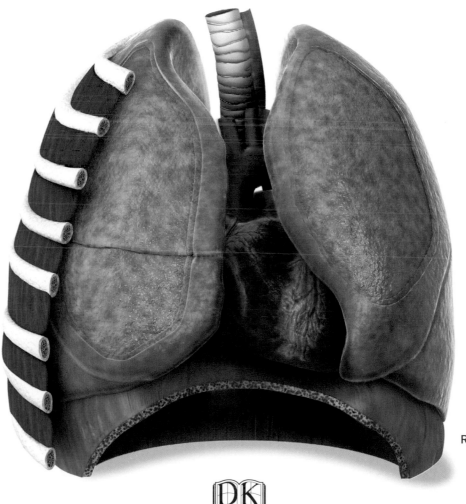

Respiratory system

DK

Chromosome

19th-century clamping forceps

Cross-section of the skin

DK

LONDON, NEW YORK, MUNICH,
MELBOURNE, AND DELHI

Editor Lisa Stock
Project editor Jane Yorke
Art editor David Ball
Senior editor Rob Houston
Senior art editor Alison Gardner
Managing editor Camilla Hallinan
Managing art editor Owen Peyton Jones
Art director Martin Wilson
Category publisher Andrew Macintyre
Picture researcher Louise Thomas
Production editor Hitesh Patel
Senior production controller Pip Tinsley
Jacket designer Andy Smith
Jacket editor Adam Powley

RELAUNCH EDITION (DK UK)
Editor Ashwin Khurana
US editor Margaret Parrish
Managing editor Gareth Jones
Managing art editor Philip Letsu
Publisher Andrew Macintyre
Producer, preproduction Nikoleta Parasaki
Senior producer Charlotte Cade
Jacket editor Maud Whatley
Jacket designer Laura Brim
Jacket design development manager Sophia MTT
Publishing director Jonathan Metcalf
Associate publishing director Liz Wheeler
Art director Phil Ormerod

RELAUNCH EDITION (DK INDIA)
Senior editor Neha Gupta
Senior art editor Ranjita Bhattacharji
Senior DTP designer Harish Aggarwal
DTP designer Pawan Kumar
Managing editor Alka Thakur Hazarika
Managing art editor Romi Chakraborty
CTS manager Balwant Singh
Jacket editorial manager Saloni Singh
Jacket designers Suhita Dharamjit, Amit Varma

First American Edition, 2009
This American Edition, 2014
Published in the United States by DK Publishing
4th floor, 345 Hudson Street, New York, New York 10014

14 15 16 17 18 10 9 8 7 6 5 4 3 2 1
001—270658—09/14

A catalog record for this book is available from the Library of Congress.

ISBN 978-1-4654-2617-8 (Paperback)
ISBN 978-1-4654-2620-8 (ALB)

DK books are available at special discounts when purchased in bulk for sales
promotions, premiums, fund-raising, or educational use. For details, contact:
DK Publishing Special Markets, 345 Hudson Street, New York, New York 10014
or SpecialSale@dk.com.

Color reproduction by Alta Image Ltd., London, UK
Printed and bound by South China Printing Co. Ltd., China

Discover more at

www.dk.com

Adult teeth

Heart

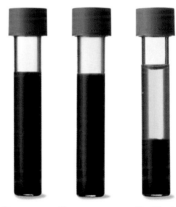

Oxygen-rich blood   Oxygen-poor blood   Settled blood

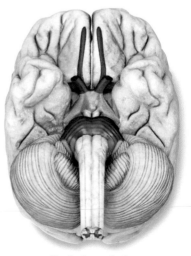

Brain from below

Contents

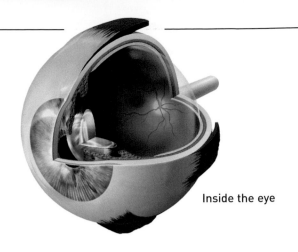

Inside the eye

The human body   6

Myth, magic, and medicine   8

Study and dissection   10

The microscopic body   12

Looking inside the body   14

The body's framework   16

Inside bones   18

The body's joints   20

Muscle power   22

The moving body   24

The nervous system   26

The brain   28

Inside the brain   30

Skin and touch   32

Eyes and seeing   34

Ears and hearing   36

Smell and taste   38

Hormones   40

The heart   42

In circulation   44

The blood   46

Breathing to live   48

Inside the lungs   50

Eating   52

Digestion   54

Waste disposal   56

Male and female   58

A new life   60

Growth and development   62

Future bodies   64

Timeline   66

Find out more   68

Glossary   70

Index   72

The human body

We may look different from the outside, but our bodies are all constructed in the same way. The study of anatomy, which explores body structure, shows that internally we are virtually identical—except for differences between males and females. The study of physiology, which deals with how the body works, reveals how body systems combine to keep our cells, and us, alive.

Human origins
Human beings are all related. We belong to the species *Homo sapiens* and are descendants of the first modern humans, who lived in Africa 160,000 years ago and migrated across the globe.

Understanding anatomy
The modern study of anatomy dates back to the Renaissance period, in the 15th and 16th centuries. For the first time, it became legal to dissect, or cut open, a dead body to examine its parts in minute detail and make accurate drawings.

Muscular system

Skeletal system

The body as a building
In 1708, physiologists likened the body to a busy household—bringing in supplies (eating food), distributing essentials (the blood system), creating warmth (body chemical processes), and organizing everyone (the brain).

Working together
Our internal organs and systems work together to keep us alive. Bones, muscles, and cartilage provide support and movement. Nerves carry control signals. The heart and blood vessels deliver food everywhere, along with oxygen taken in through the lungs. The result of this cooperation is a balanced internal environment, with a constant temperature of 98.6°F (37°C). This enables cells to work at their best.

Eye is a light-detecting sense organ

Vein carries the blood toward the heart

Artery carries the blood away from the heart

Nerve carries electrical signals to and from the brain

Bone supports the upper arm

Body makeup

It takes around 100 trillion cells to build a human body. There are 200 different types of these microscopic living units, each of which is highly complex. Similar cells join together to make a tissue, two or more tissues form an organ, and linked organs create a system. The body has 12 systems.

Cartilage supports the nose

Teeth cut up food during eating

Neck muscle moves the head

Lung gets oxygen into the body

Heart pumps the blood

Tendon attaches a muscle to bone

Liver cleans the blood

1 System
Along with the digestive system, the other 11 are the skin, skeletal, muscular, nervous, hormonal, circulatory, lymphatic, immune, respiratory, urinary, and reproductive systems. The role of the digestive system is to break down food so it can be used by body cells.

Small intestine

Digestive system

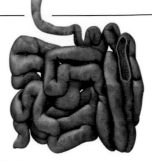

2 Organ
The small intestine is a long digestive tube. It completes the breakdown of food into simple substances, which are absorbed into the blood. Muscle tissue in the wall of the small intestine pushes food along it.

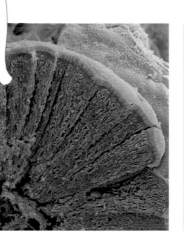

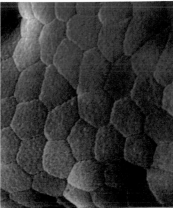

3 Tissue
The lining of the small intestine has millions of microscopic fingerlike projections called villi. This epithelial tissue provides a vast surface for absorbing food.

4 Cells
The epithelial cells covering a villus are tightly clumped together, which stops food and digestive juices from leaking through to the tissues that support these cells.

5 Chromosome
Every cell has a control center, called its nucleus, which contains 46 chromosomes. These long threads (coiled up in an X-shape, above) contain coded instructions, called genes, which are needed for building our cells, tissues, organs, and systems.

6 DNA
Each chromosome consists of deoxyribonucleic acid (DNA), a molecule. DNA's twisted strands are linked by chemicals called bases (blue, green, red, yellow). Their sequence provides a gene's coded instructions for building or controlling the body.

Myth, magic, and medicine

Early humans made sculptures and cave paintings of human figures. As civilizations grew, people began to study the world around them and their own bodies more closely, but care for the sick and injured was tied up with myths, superstition, and a belief that gods or demons sent illnesses. The "father of medicine," Greek physician Hippocrates (c. 460–377 BCE) taught that diseases could be identified and treated. In the Roman world, Galen (129–c. 216 CE) set out ideas about anatomy and physiology that would last for centuries. As Rome's power declined, medical knowledge spread east to Persia, developed by physicians such as Avicenna (980–1037 CE).

Prehistoric art
The Aboriginal rock art of Australia has featured X-ray figures showing the internal anatomy of humans and animals for 4,000 years.

Holes in the head
This 4,000-year-old skull from Jericho, in Israel, shows the results of trepanning, or drilling holes in the skull—probably to expose the brain and release evil spirits. Modern surgery uses a similar technique, called craniotomy, to release pressure in the brain caused by bleeding.

Surgical sacrifice
In the 14th and 15th centuries, the Aztecs who dominated Mexico believed the god Huitzilopochtli would make the Sun rise and bring them success in battle, if offered daily blood, limbs, and hearts torn from living human sacrifices. From these grisly rituals, the Aztecs learned about the inner organs of the body.

Egyptian embalming
Some 5,000 years ago, the Egyptians believed that a dead body remained home to its owner's soul in the afterlife, but only if preserved as a lifelike mummy. Natron, a type of salt, was used to dry out the body to embalm it and stop it from rotting.

Internal organs, removed from an opening in the side, were preserved separately in special jars

Brain, regarded as useless, was hooked out through the nostrils and discarded

Heart, seen as the center of being, was left inside the chest

Chinese channels

Written over 2,300 years ago, *The Yellow Emperor's Classic of Internal Medicine* explains acupuncture treatments, which focus on the flow of chi, or vital energy, along 12 body channels, or meridians. Needles are inserted into the skin along these meridians to rebalance the body forces known as Yin (cool and female) and Yang (hot and male).

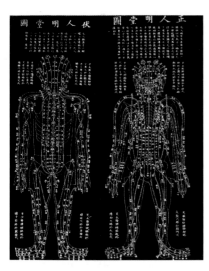

Galen remained a great influence in Europe and the Islamic world for many centuries

Medieval treatments

Blood letting, using a knife or a bloodsucking worm called a leech, was a traditional, if brutal, remedy for all manner of ills in medieval times. Few physicians tried to see if the treatment was of any benefit to the patient

Embalming process dried out the muscles, which shrank and exposed the bones

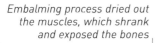

Claudius Galen

Born in ancient Greece, Claudius Galen became a towering figure in the study of anatomy, physiology, and medicine in Rome. There, he treated gladiators as a young physician, describing their wounds as "windows into the body." Human dissection was banned, so he studied the anatomy of animals instead. His flawed ideas were accepted without question for 1,500 years.

Hippocrates believed that physicians should act in their patients' best interests

Saving knowledge

This illustration comes from the 1610 translation of the *Canon Of Medicine*, written by the Persian physician Avicenna in c. 1025. He built on the knowledge of Galen and Hippocrates, whose medical works survived the fall of Rome only because they were taken to Persia, translated, and spread through the Islamic world. Their ideas were reintroduced to Europe after Islam spread to Spain in 711 CE.

Avicenna, the Persian anatomist, built on the teachings of the Romans and Greeks

Skin became dark and leathery through embalming and age

Toenails, being made of dead cells, remained intact

Study and dissection

Respect for death
For many in the Middle Ages, life was less important than death and ascent into heaven. It was thought that the body housed the soul and should not be dissected. An anatomist risked punishment.

A rebirth of the arts, architecture, and science spread across Europe between the 14th and 17th centuries. With the dawn of this Renaissance, the ban on human dissection—the precise cutting open of a body to study its internal structure—was relaxed. In Italy, Andreas Vesalius (1514–64) performed careful, accurate dissections and drew his own conclusions, based on his observations, rather than blindly repeating the centuries-old accepted views. By questioning and correcting Galen's teachings, he revolutionized the science of anatomy and initiated a new era in medicine.

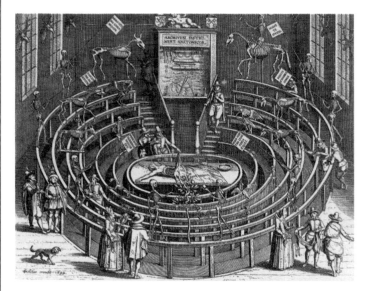

Anatomical theater
Mondino dei Liuzzi (c. 1270–1326), a professor at Bologna, Italy, introduced the public dissection of human corpses and is known as the Restorer of Anatomy. By the late 16th century, anatomical theaters were built at numerous universities. This 1610 engraving shows the anatomical theater at Leiden, in the Netherlands. Spectators in the gallery looked down as the anatomy professor or his assistant performed a dissection.

Strong, thick metal frame

End screw to remove blade

Break with tradition
Padua was at the forefront of Italian anatomy and medicine when Andreas Vesalius arrived in 1536. His exceptional skills were soon evident, and he soon became professor of anatomy. After translating early medical texts, Vesalius became dissatisfied with the teachings of ancient times. He preferred to believe what he saw in front of him and set about writing his own book.

First scientific anatomy book
After four years of dissection Vesalius's *On the Structure of the Human Body* was published in 1543. The detailed text and lifelike-in-death illustrations caused sensation and outrage.

Subjects for study

Hanged criminals were a steady source of specimens for dissection. In *The Anatomy Lesson of Dr. Nicholaes Tulp* (1632), by the Dutch artist Rembrandt, the dissection subject was robber Aris Kindt. Anatomy lessons were training for physicians and surgeons and were open to any interested members of the public.

Women and anatomy

Until the 19th century, women took on only very minor medical roles, except as midwifes. These Swedish women learning anatomy, in a photograph from about 1880, are probably training for midwifery.

Fine end

Double-ended small probe

Bulbous end

Hooked point   **Hooked needle**   *Wooden handle*

Blade can be sharpened for use

Skull removed to expose brain

Scalpel

Needlelike tips

Fine forceps (tweezers)

Ridged, splayed tips for gripping

Clamping forceps

Handles have a scissor design

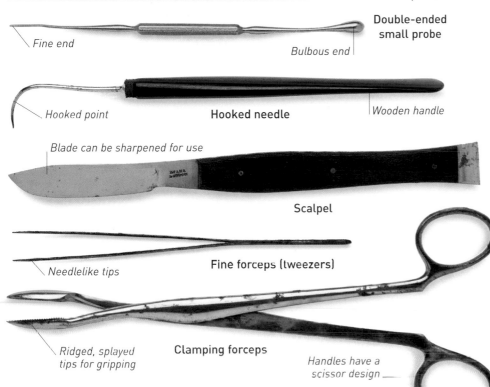

Muscle layer peeled back

Tools of the trade

These 19th-century surgical instruments each have their own role, from cutting through bones to probing tiny nerves and blood vessels. Today's surgeons use a similar but broader range of instruments, making use of modern technology, such as power saws and laser scalpels.

Wax model

Crafted from wax, this anatomical model shows the dissected head and neck, including muscles, nerves, blood vessels, and the brain. In the 18th and 19th centuries, accurately colored, three-dimensional models like this one were excellent teaching aids for trainee doctors.

Instruments illustrated in the second edition of Vesalius's book, 1555

Serrated saw blade

Large bone saw

Tensioning screw to tighten blade

Wooden handle shaped to fit palm of hand

The microscopic body

At the beginning of the 1600s, scientific instrument makers in the Netherlands invented a magnifying device called the microscope. For the first time, scientists used high-quality glass lenses to view objects, illuminated by light, which previously had been far too small to see with the naked eye. Pioneering microscopists showed that living things are made up of much smaller units, which Robert Hooke (1635–1703) likened to the cells, or rooms, of monks in a monastery. The term "cells" has been used ever since.

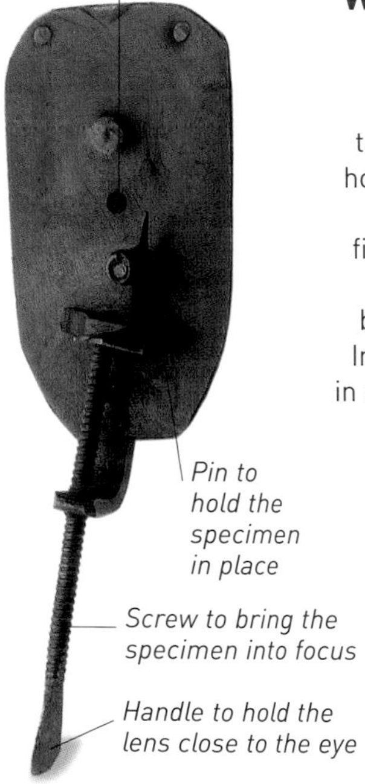

Pioneer histologist

Italy's Marcello Malpighi (1628–94) was the founder of microscopic anatomy and a pioneer of histology, the study of tissues. He was the first to identify capillaries, the tiny blood vessels that connect arteries to veins.

Lens held between two plates

Wide-ranging observer

Antoni van Leeuwenhoek (1632–1723) was a Dutch cloth merchant and self-taught scientist. With his homemade microscopes Leeuwenhoek was the first to observe, among many other things, blood cells and sperm. In 1683 he also spotted, in scrapings from his own teeth, the first bacteria seen by the human eye.

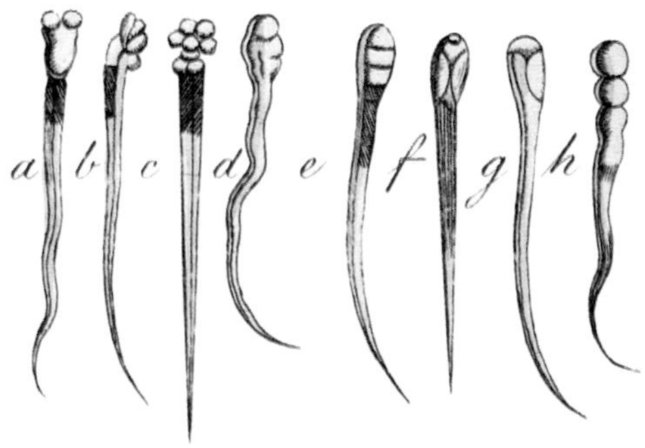

Pin to hold the specimen in place

Screw to bring the specimen into focus

Handle to hold the lens close to the eye

Homemade lenses

In van Leeuwenhoek's day, most microscopes had two lenses, as shown on the right. His version, shown life-sized above, had one tiny lens, yet it enabled him to observe cells, tissues, and tiny organisms magnified up to 275 times. He made about 400 microscopes, and he helped to establish microscopy as a branch of science.

Microscopic drawings

Today, photography can capture what is viewed under the microscope. Early microscopists used drawings and writing to record what they saw. This drawing by van Leeuwenhoek records his observation, for the first time, of sperm cells.

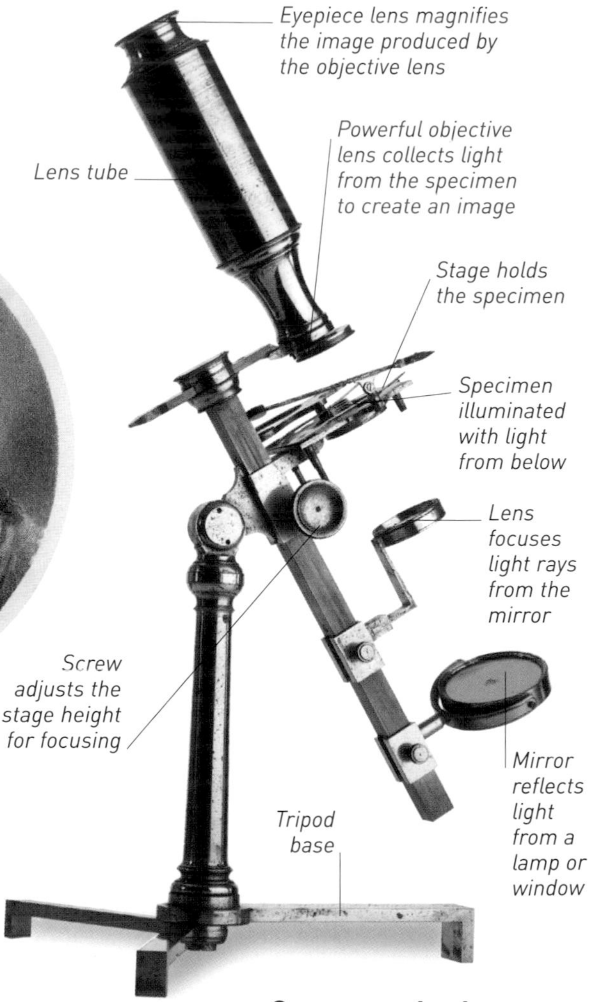

Eyepiece lens magnifies the image produced by the objective lens

Lens tube

Powerful objective lens collects light from the specimen to create an image

Stage holds the specimen

Specimen illuminated with light from below

Lens focuses light rays from the mirror

Screw adjusts the stage height for focusing

Mirror reflects light from a lamp or window

Tripod base

Compound microscope

Van Leeuwenhoek's "simple" microscopes had only one lens. Most light microscopes, which use light for illuminating the specimen, are compound, using two or more lenses. This 19th-century model has the basic features found on a modern compound microscope. The specimen is sliced thinly enough for light to be shone through it and up through the lenses to the eye.

Inside a cell

This cutaway model of a typical human cell shows the parts of a cell that can be seen using an electron microscope. A thin cell membrane surrounds the cell. The jellylike cytoplasm contains organelles (small organs), each with a supporting role. The nucleus, the largest structure within the cell, contains the instructions needed to run the cell.

Electron gun

Electron microscope

An electron microscope uses minute parts of atoms called electrons to magnify thousands or millions of times. Focused by magnets, an electron beam is fired toward a specimen at the base. Electrons that pass through or bounce off the specimen are detected and create an image on a monitor.

Organelles called endoplasmic reticulum transport proteins for cell metabolism

Nucleus is the cell's control center

Organelles called mitochondria provide energy for metabolism

Microtubule supports and shapes the cell

Organelle called the Golgi body processes proteins for use inside or outside the cell

Cell membrane controls movement of substances in and out of the cell

Cytoplasm in which the organelles float and move

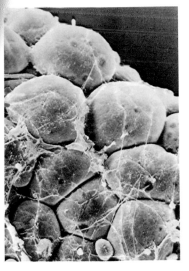

Surface view

In a scanning electron microscope, an electron beam scans the surface of a whole specimen. Electrons bouncing off the specimen are focused to produce a black-and-white, three-dimensional image. This scanning electron micrograph (SEM) shows fat cells.

Cell slice

A transmission electron microscope projects an electron beam through a slice of body tissue onto a monitor. The image is photographed to produce a transmission electron micrograph. This TEM shows a liver cell's mitochondria (white), and endoplasmic reticulum (blue).

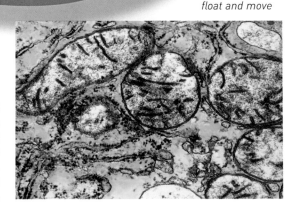

Looking inside the body

In the past, the only way to see inside the body was to cut it open or inspect soldiers' wounds. The invention of the ophthalmoscope in 1851 allowed doctors to view the inside of a patient's eye for the first time. In 1895, X-rays were discovered and used to produce images of bones without cutting open the body. Today's imaging techniques allow us to view tissues, search for signs of disease, and find out how the body works.

War wounds
This illustration from a German medical manual of 1540 shows surgeons how to extract an arrowhead from a soldier on the battlefield.

Screw widens nose-piece to hold open nostril

Nasal speculum for examining the nose

Screws onto the otoscope here

Angled mirror to reflect the view

Rotating set of magnifying lenses for examining the eye

Finger bones are clearly visible

Mirror head for the laryngoscope

Tongue depressor for the laryngoscope

Head attachments screw on here

Light source in the tip

Funnel-shaped tip inserted into the outer ear canal

Metal rings and key chain

Mysterious rays
This radiograph from 1896 was produced by projecting X-rays (a form of radiation) through a woman's hand onto a photographic plate. Hard bones and metal show up clearly since they absorb X-rays that pass through softer tissues.

Otoscope head for examining inside the ear

Handle

Laryngoscope head for examining the throat

CT scanning
A computed tomography (CT) scan uses X-rays and a computer to look inside the body. A patient lies inside a rotating scanner, which sends a narrow beam of X-rays through the body to a detector. The result is a two-dimensional slice of the body showing hard and soft tissues. A computer combines image slices together to build up a three-dimensional picture of a body part, such as this living heart.

Medical viewing kit
Today's doctors routinely use this multipurpose medical equipment when examining patients. The kit consists of a handle, which contains batteries to power a light source, and a range of attachments used for looking inside the ears, throat, nose, or eyes. For example, using the ophthalmoscope attachment, a doctor can shine a light and look into a patient's eye.

Opthalmoscope

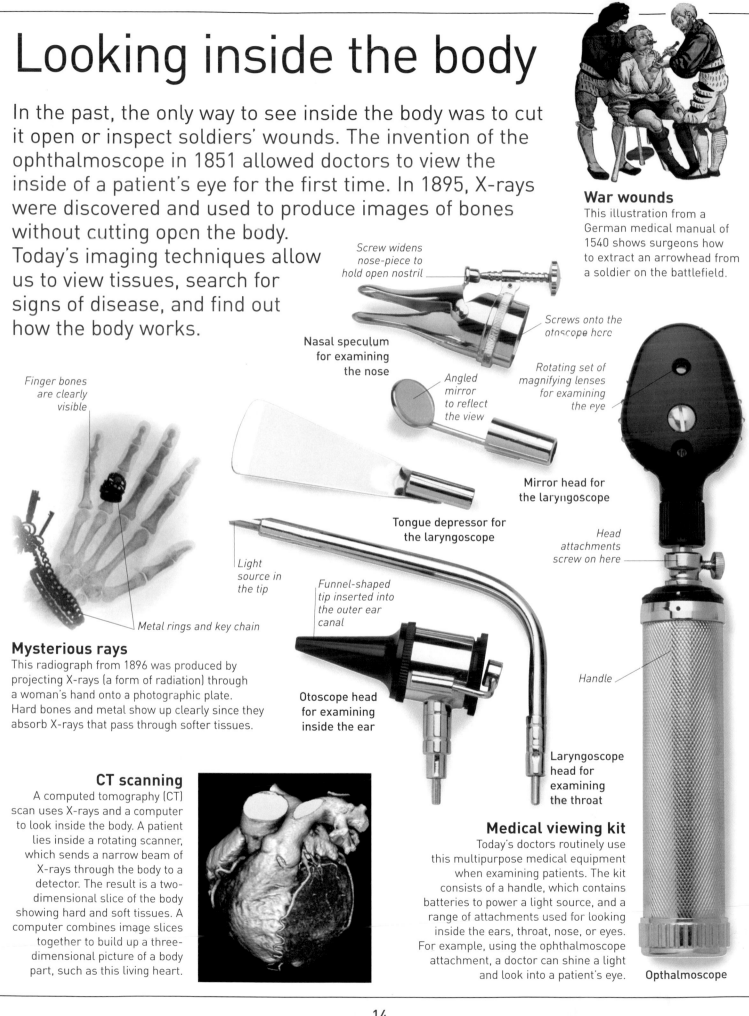

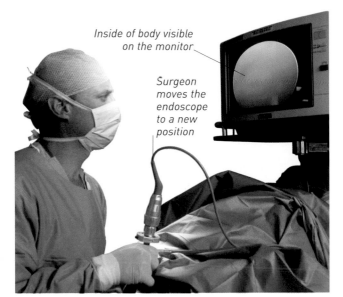

Inside of body visible on the monitor

Surgeon moves the endoscope to a new position

Endoscope

Surgeons use a thin, tubelike endoscope to examine tissues and to look inside joints. It is inserted via a natural body opening, such as the mouth, or a small incision in the skin (as shown here). Optical fibers inside the tube carry bright light to illuminate the inside of the body and send back images to a monitor.

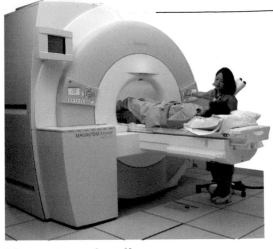

Magnets and radio waves

Inside a magnetic resonance imaging (MRI) scanner, a powerful magnetic field lines up the hydrogen atoms in the patient's body. Bursts of radio waves knock the atoms back into position. When the magnetic field lines the atoms up again, they send out tiny radio signals. Different tissues and organs send out differing signals that are detected and turned into images by a computer.

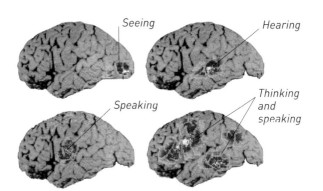

Seeing

Hearing

Speaking

Thinking and speaking

Brain tissue at work

Positron emission tomography (PET) scans reveal how active specific body tissues are. First, a form of glucose (sugar) is injected into the bloodstream to provide food energy for hardworking tissues. As the tissues consume the glucose, particles are released that can be detected to form an image.

Brain inside the skull

Left lung inside the chest

Full body scan

This MRI scan shows a vertical cross-section through a man's body. This is produced by combining many individual scans made along the length of the body. The original black-and-white image has been color enhanced to highlight different tissues and organs.

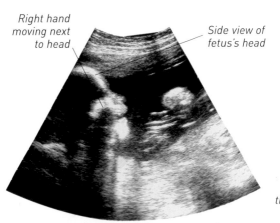

Right hand moving next to head

Side view of fetus's head

Urinary bladder in the lower abdomen

Fleshy calf muscle in the lower leg

Femur (thigh bone) extends from the hip to the knee

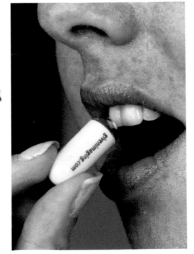

Video pill

This capsule endoscope can be used to identify damage or disease in the digestive system. It contains a tiny camera, light source, and transmitter. Once swallowed, it travels along the digestive system, taking pictures that are then transmitted to an outside receiver for a doctor to view.

From echo to image

Ultrasound scanning produces moving images such as this fetus inside the womb. High-pitched sound waves are beamed into the body, reflected back by tissues, and converted into images by a computer.

The body's framework

The skeleton's 206 bones make up a hard yet flexible framework that supports and shapes the body. It surrounds and protects organs such as the brain and heart and stops them from being jolted or crushed. Bones also provide anchorage for the muscles that move the skeleton and, therefore, the whole body. Unlike early anatomists, today's scientists can examine bones inside a living body.

Symbol of death
Skeletons are enduring symbols of danger, disease, death, and destruction—as seen in this 15th-century *Dance of Death* drawing.

Understanding bones
For centuries, bones were regarded as lifeless supports for the active, softer tissues around them. Gradually, anatomists saw that bones were alive, with their own blood vessels and nerves. Here, the renowned medieval surgeon Guy de Chauliac, author of *Great Surgery* (1363), examines a fracture, or broken bone.

Body mechanics
Many machines copy principles of mechanics shown by the skeleton. For example, each arm has two sets of long bones that can extend the reach of the hand, or fold back on themselves—like these cranes.

Spinal cord is protected by the vertebrae

Model backbone
The backbone, or spine, is a strong, flexible column of 33 vertebrae that keeps the body upright. Each vertebra has a centrum, which bears the body's weight. A pad of cartilage forms a cushion between one centrum and the next. This allows limited movement between neighboring vertebrae. All of these tiny movements added together along the length of the backbone enable the body to bend forward, backward, side to side, and to twist.

Centrum (body) of the vertebra

Intervertebral disk of cartilage

Lumbar (lower back) section of the spine

Spinous process (bump) for muscle attachment

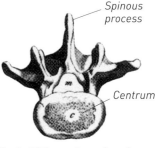

Spinous process

Centrum

Early 19th-century drawing of a lumbar vertebra, seen from above

Talus connects to tibia (shinbone) and fibula

Tarsals (ankle bones)

Metatarsals (sole bones)

Calcaneus (heel bone)

Phalanges (toe bones) of smaller toe

Phalanges of big toe

Bones of the foot
The feet bear the whole weight of the body and each one is made up of 26 bones: seven in the ankle, five in the sole, and three in each toe, except for the big toe, which has two.

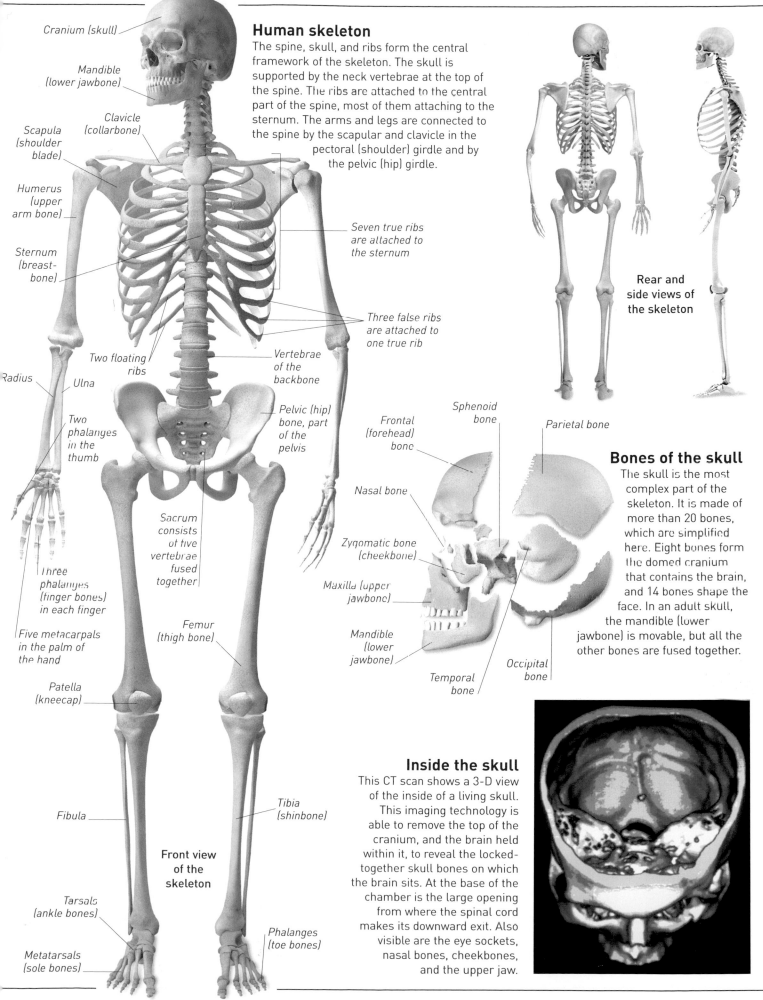

Cranium (skull)

Mandible (lower jawbone)

Clavicle (collarbone)

Scapula (shoulder blade)

Humerus (upper arm bone)

Sternum (breast-bone)

Radius

Ulna

Two phalanges in the thumb

Three phalanges (finger bones) in each finger

Five metacarpals in the palm of the hand

Patella (kneecap)

Fibula

Tarsals (ankle bones)

Metatarsals (sole bones)

Human skeleton

The spine, skull, and ribs form the central framework of the skeleton. The skull is supported by the neck vertebrae at the top of the spine. The ribs are attached to the central part of the spine, most of them attaching to the sternum. The arms and legs are connected to the spine by the scapular and clavicle in the pectoral (shoulder) girdle and by the pelvic (hip) girdle.

Seven true ribs are attached to the sternum

Three false ribs are attached to one true rib

Two floating ribs

Vertebrae of the backbone

Pelvic (hip) bone, part of the pelvis

Sacrum consists of five vertebrae fused together

Femur (thigh bone)

Tibia (shinbone)

Front view of the skeleton

Phalanges (toe bones)

Rear and side views of the skeleton

Frontal (forehead) bone

Sphenoid bone

Parietal bone

Nasal bone

Zygomatic bone (cheekbone)

Maxilla (upper jawbone)

Mandible (lower jawbone)

Temporal bone

Occipital bone

Bones of the skull

The skull is the most complex part of the skeleton. It is made of more than 20 bones, which are simplified here. Eight bones form the domed cranium that contains the brain, and 14 bones shape the face. In an adult skull, the mandible (lower jawbone) is movable, but all the other bones are fused together.

Inside the skull

This CT scan shows a 3-D view of the inside of a living skull. This imaging technology is able to remove the top of the cranium, and the brain held within it, to reveal the locked-together skull bones on which the brain sits. At the base of the chamber is the large opening from where the spinal cord makes its downward exit. Also visible are the eye sockets, nasal bones, cheekbones, and the upper jaw.

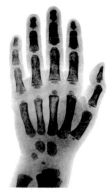

Inside bones

Our bones are living organs with a complex structure of hard bone tissues, blood vessels, and nerves. Bone is as strong as steel, but only one-sixth its weight. Each bone also has a slight springiness that enables it to withstand knocks and jolts, usually without breaking. Tough, dense bony tissue, called compact bone, surrounds light-but-strong spongy bone inside—otherwise the skeleton would be too heavy for the body to move.

Growing bone
In a young embryo the skeleton forms from flexible cartilage, which turns into bone over time. This X-ray of a young child's hand shows growing bones (dark blue) and spaces where cartilage will be replaced.

Rope and pulley moves broken bones back into position

Setting bones
Skeletons of 100,000 years ago show that broken bones were set, or repositioned, to aid healing. Here, 17th-century surgeons are setting a broken arm.

Resisting pressure
When weight is put on a bone, its structure prevents it from bending. For example, in the hip joint (shown here in cross-section) the head and neck of the femur (thighbone) bear the full weight of the body. The largest area of bone consists of spongy bone, in which the trabeculae, or framework of struts, are lined up to resist downward force. The thin covering of compact bone resists squashing on one side of the femur and stretching on the opposite side.

Pelvic (hip) bone

Head and neck of the femur (thighbone)

Spongy bone

Compact bone resists squashing

Inside a long bone
In the cutaway below, compact bone forms the hard outer layer. It is made up of parallel bundles of osteons (see opposite) that run lengthwise and act as weight-bearing pillars. Inside is lighter spongy bone and a central, marrow-filled cavity.

Compact bone resists stretching

Muscle

Spongy bone
This SEM of spongy, or cancellous, bone shows an open framework of struts and spaces, or trabeculae. In living bone these form a structure of great strength and the spaces are filled with bone marrow. Spongy bone is lighter than compact bone, and so reduces the overall weight of a bone.

Head of bone is mostly spongy bone

Artery supplies oxygen-rich blood to the bone cells

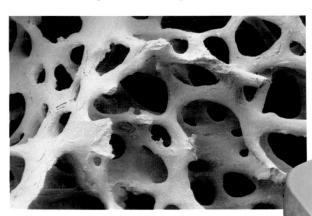

Bone expert

Italy's Giovanni Ingrassias (1510–80) was a founder of osteology, or the study of bones. His research corrected many mistaken ideas about bones. Ingrassias also identified the body's smallest bone, the stapes (stirrup) of the ear, and he described the arrangement of skull bones that form part of the eye socket.

Bone microstructure

This model shows a microscopic view of a slice of compact bone, made up of layered osteons measuring just 0.25 mm across. Blood vessels run through their central canal, supplying food and oxygen to the bone cells to maintain the bone framework. This is made of bendy fibers of the protein collagen and hard minerals, mainly calcium phosphate, which make the bone strong but not brittle.

Osteon

Lamellae (layered tubes) of the osteon

Blood vessel

Outer lamellae strengthen the whole bone

Osteocyte (bone cell)

Bone cells

This SEM shows an osteocyte (bone cell) in a lacuna—a tiny space in the framework of minerals and fibers that makes up compact bone. Osteocytes are linked by strandlike extensions of their cell bodies that pass along the narrow canals inside bone.

Periosteum

Central canal of the osteon

Branch of blood vessel between the osteons

Spongy bone

Bone marrow

Jellylike bone marrow fills the spaces inside spongy bone and the central cavity of long bones. As the body grows, bone-cell-making red marrow is gradually replaced by fat-storing yellow marrow. In adults, red bone marrow remains only in a few bones, such as the skull, spine, and breastbone. These sites release more than two million red blood cells per second into the bloodstream.

Periosteum, a thin, fibrous membrane covering the bone

Head of bone

Rich network of blood vessels nourishes the bone

Compact bone is the hard, dense outer layer of the bone

Bone shaft

Osteon is one of the layered tubes that make up compact bone

Central cavity

Vein carries oxygen-poor blood away from the bone cells

Yellow bone marrow fills the central cavity and stores fat

Making new blood cells

This SEM shows red bone marrow, where blood cells are made. Unspecialized stem cells multiply to produce cells that rapidly multiply again to form billions of red blood cells (red) and white blood cells (blue).

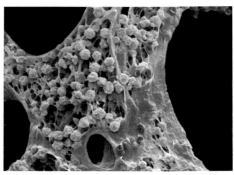

The body's joints

Wherever two or more bones meet in the skeleton, they form a joint. Most of the body's 400-plus joints, such as those in our fingers and toes, are synovial, or freely movable. There are several types of movable joint, held together by ligaments, which makes the skeleton incredibly flexible. Without them, it would be rigid.

Supple joints
Joints benefit from use and deteriorate with neglect. Activities such as yoga promote the full range of joint movement and enjoy maximum flexibility.

Pivot joint allows the head to shake

Condyloid joint allows the head to nod

Hinge joint allows the arm to bend at the elbow

Simple hinge joints between the phalanges (finger bones) enable the fingers to bend in two places

Condyloid joint is an oval ball-and-socket joint allowing the fingers to swivel, but not to rotate

Palm of hand extends to the knuckles

Gliding joints allow limited sliding movements between the eight bones of the wrist

Saddle joint gives thumb great flexibility and a delicate touch when picking up tiny objects with the fingers

Limb can move in many directions

Femur (thighbone)

Pelvic (hip) bone

Ball-and-socket joint in the hip

Femur (thighbone)

Tibia (shinbone)

Hinge joint in the knee

Limb moves back and forth in one direction

Balls, sockets, and hinges
The hip and knee's movements can be seen whenever someone climbs, walks, dances, or kicks. The hip joint is a ball-and-socket joint. The rounded end of the thighbone swivels in the cup-shaped socket in the hip bone and permits movement in all directions, including rotation. The knee is a hinge joint and moves mainly in one front-to-back direction.

Gliding joint allows the kneecap to move away from the femur (thighbone) as the knee bends

Hinge joint allows the foot to bend at the ankle

Joints galore
With its 27 bones and 19 movable joints, the hand can perform many delicate tasks. The first knuckle joint of each digit (finger) is condyloid—it and the other hinge joints allow the fingers to curl around and grasp objects. The saddle joint at the base of the thumb—the most mobile digit—allows it to swing across the palm and touch the tips of the other fingers for a precise grip.

Versatile mover
The skeleton is extremely flexible because it contains many different types of joint, each permitting different ranges of movement. Ball-and-socket, condyloid, and saddle joints allow flexible movements in several directions. Others are more limited. Pivot joints allow movement from side to side, hinge joints back and forth, and gliding joints enable small sliding movements between bones.

Binding the bones

Tough straps of strong, elastic tissue called ligaments surround bone ends in a joint—such as the ankle—and bind them together securely to prevent them from moving excessively.

Tibia (shinbone)

Fibula

Ligament linking the calcaneus and fibula

Calcaneus (heel bone)

Pivot joint permits the forearm to twist

Gliding joint between the rib and backbone

Saddle joint gives the thumb great mobility

Condyloid joint gives the wrist flexibility

Ligament linking the tibia and fibula

Tarsal (ankle bone)

Ligaments connecting the tarsals and metatarsals

Metatarsals (sole bones)

Ball-and-socket joint between the femur (thighbone) and hip enables the leg to move in all directions

Hinge joint allows the leg to bend at the knee

Gliding joint between the tarsals (ankle bones) allows little movement, which strengthens the ankle

Condyloid joint allows the toes to bend and wiggle

Hinge joint allows the toe to bend

Inside a synovial joint

This view into a typical, movable joint shows its main parts. Inside the protective joint capsule and ligaments is the synovial membrane. This makes synovial fluid, the oil that lubricates the joint. The bone ends are covered by friction-reducing, shiny hyaline cartilage.

Bone marrow

Bone

Joint capsule

Synovial fluid

Synovial membrane

Hyaline cartilage

Ligaments

Cartilage

Tough and flexible, cartilage is a supporting tissue that resists pushing and pulling forces. There are three types. Hyaline cartilage covers bone ends to help joints move smoothly. It also, among other things, connects the ribs to the sternum. Elastic cartilage is strong and stretchy. It supports the outside of the ear, for example. Fibrocartilage can withstand heavy pressure and is found in the disks between vertebrae in the backbone and in the knee joints.

Cartilage cells

Cells called chondrocytes make cartilage around themselves. It consists of two types of fibers—the tough protein collagen and the elastic protein elastin, woven together into a stiff jelly with water. Nutrients seep into cartilage cells from the blood vessels that run around its edges.

Chondrocyte

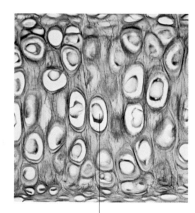

Knee trouble

The knee is the body's biggest joint. It is strengthened by ligaments inside the joint, and cushioned from jolts by pads of cartilage called the menisci. Sports such as soccer involve rapid turns and high kicks, which can cause knee injuries.

Muscle power

Muscle tissue pulls—and generates movement—by contracting, or getting shorter. Skeletal muscles make up nearly half the body's total mass. They shape the body and, by pulling on bones, hold it upright to maintain posture and allow it to perform a wide range of movements from blinking to running. The two other muscle types are smooth and cardiac muscle. Most muscles have Latin names that describe their location, size, shape, or action.

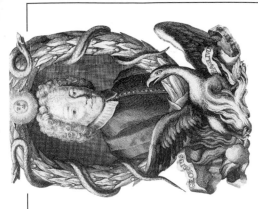

The ultimate book

Italian anatomist Giorgio Baglivi (1668–1707) was the first to note that skeletal muscles differ from the muscles working the intestines and other organs.

Under the microscope

Danish scientist and bishop Nicholas Steno (1638–86) looked at muscles with a microscope and found that their contraction was due to the shortening of the thousands of tiny fibers that make up each muscle.

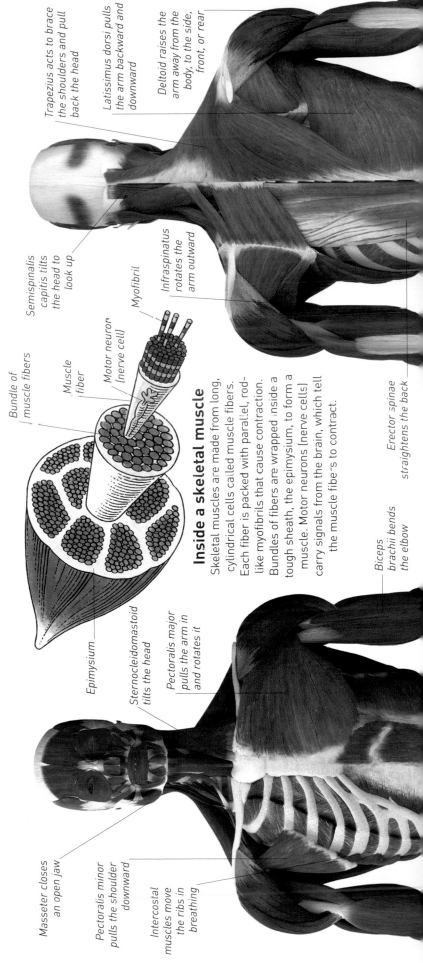

Trapezius acts to brace the shoulders and pull back the head

Latissimus dorsi pulls the arm backward and downward

Deltoid raises the arm away from the body, to the side, front, or rear

Semispinalis capitis tilts the head to look up

Infraspinatus rotates the arm outward

Bundle of muscle fibers

Muscle fiber

Motor neuron (nerve cell)

Myofibril

Inside a skeletal muscle

Skeletal muscles are made from long, cylindrical cells called muscle fibers. Each fiber is packed with parallel, rod-like myofibrils that cause contraction. Bundles of fibers are wrapped inside a tough sheath, the epimysium, to form a muscle. Motor neurons (nerve cells) carry signals from the brain, which tell the muscle fibers to contract.

Erector spinae straightens the back

Biceps brachii bends the elbow

Epimysium

Sternocleidomastoid tilts the head

Pectoralis major pulls the arm in and rotates it

Masseter closes an open jaw

Pectoralis minor pulls the shoulder downward

Intercostal muscles move the ribs in breathing

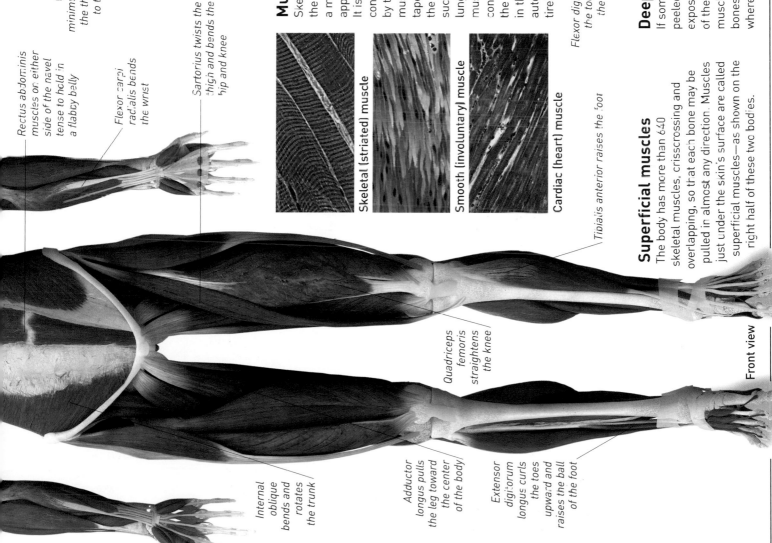

Gluteus maximus straightens the hip

Biceps femoris, one of the hamstrings, bends the knee

Gastrocnemius lifts the heel and bends the knee

Calcaneal (Achilles) tendon, the body's biggest, attaches the calf muscles to the heel bone

Tibialis posterior counteracts sway when standing on one foot

Flexor hallucis longus curls the sole and toes downward

Rear view

Gluteus minimus pulls the thigh out to the side

Rectus abdominis muscles on either side of the navel tense to hold in a flabby belly

Flexor carpi radialis bends the wrist

Sartorius twists the thigh and bends the hip and knee

Muscle types

Skeletal muscle moves the bones. Seen under a microscope, its fibers appear striated (striped). It is a voluntary muscle, contracting when told to by the brain. Smooth muscle, with its sheets of tapering fibers, is found in the walls of hollow organs such as the intestines and lungs. This involuntary muscle works without the conscious involvement of the brain. Cardiac muscle, in the heart, contracts automatically and tirelessly for a lifetime.

Skeletal (striated) muscle

Smooth (involuntary) muscle

Cardiac (heart) muscle

Deep muscles

If some superficial muscles are peeled away, deeper muscles are exposed—as shown on the left half of these bodies. Many of these muscles lie directly next to the bones they pull, and the points where they join may be visible.

Flexor digitorum longus bends the toes downward to help the foot grip the ground

Superficial muscles

The body has more than 640 skeletal muscles, crisscrossing and overlapping, so that each bone may be pulled in almost any direction. Muscles just under the skin's surface are called superficial muscles—as shown on the right half of these two bodies.

Tibialis anterior raises the foot

Internal oblique bends and rotates the trunk

Adductor longus pulls the leg toward the center of the body

Extensor digitorum longus curls the toes upward and raises the ball of the foot

Quadriceps femoris straightens the knee

Front view

The moving body

Muscles are attached to bones by tough, fibrous cords called tendons. When muscles contract (get shorter), they pull on a bone. The bone that moves when the muscle contracts is called the insertion and the other bone, which stays still, is called the origin. Muscles can only pull, not push, so moving a body part in different directions requires opposing pairs of muscles.

The three S-words
Muscle fitness can be assessed by strength, stamina, and suppleness. Swimming and dancing promote all three.

Neck muscles bend the head back

Muscles in the back of the forearm extend (straighten) the fingers

Extensor tendon to the index finger

Phalanges (finger bones)

Transverse ligament stops the tendons moving sideways

Biceps contracted

Triceps relaxed

Triceps contracted

Back muscles arch the back

Raised forearm

Flexed elbow

Extensor retinaculum holds the long tendons in place

Biceps relaxed

Separate extensor tendons begin at the end of the extensor digitorum

Elbow straight

Forearm lowered

Muscle pairs
Muscles can only contract and pull, so moving a body part in opposite directions requires two different muscles. Many muscles are arranged in opposing pairs. In the arm, the biceps pulls the forearm upward and bends the elbow, while its opposing partner, the triceps, pulls the forearm downward and straightens the elbow.

Extensor digitorum straightens the fingers when it contracts

Tendons
Many of the muscles that move the fingers are not in the hand, but in the forearm. They work the fingers by remote control, using long tendons extending from the ends of the muscles to attach to the bones that they move. The tendons run smoothly in slippery tendon sheaths that reduce wear.

Power and precision
With practice, pianists can train their brains to coordinate complex, rhythmic movements in all 10 fingers. Muscles work the flexible framework of 27 bones in each hand to play notes ranging from delicate to explosive.

Working together

To perform the pose below, areas of the brain that control movement and balance send out nerve signals to instruct specific skeletal muscles when to contract and by how much. Muscles in the hands, arms, torso, and legs work together to put the gymnast in this position. Signals from the muscles and tendons also feed back to the brain so that minor adjustments maintain her balance.

Calf muscles bend the foot downward to point the toes

Hand muscles pull the fingers together

Muscles at the back of the thigh pull the leg backward

Muscle at the front of the thigh pulls the leg forward and straightens the knee

Pairs of muscles at the front and back of the leg tense to keep balance

Old theories

Dutch physician Jan Swammerdam (1637–90) disproved ideas that a vital spirit passed along nerves and inflated muscles to make them contract. He showed that muscles altered in shape, but not in volume (the space they take up) during contraction.

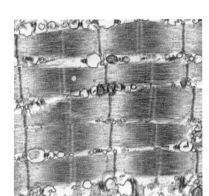

Myofibril contraction

This TEM shows myofibrils, the long cylinders that extend the length of a skeletal muscle fiber, or cell. Here, running from left to right, they are divided into units between the thin, vertical lines. Each unit contains thick and thin filaments, producing the blue-and-pink pattern. The thick and thin filaments slide over each other, making the myofibril—and the entire muscle—shorter.

Frontalis raises the eyebrows and wrinkles the forehead

Orbicularis oculi closes the eye

Corrugator supercilii pulls the eyebrows together

Levator labii superioris lifts and curls the upper lip

Orbicularis oris closes, purses, and protrudes the lips—during a kiss, for example

Mentalis protrudes the lower lip

Depressor anguli oris pulls down the corner of the mouth

Temporalis lifts the lower jaw, during biting, for example

Face, head, and neck

From frowning to smiling, around 30 facial muscles produce the great variety of expressions. These muscles are also involved in activities such as blinking and chewing. They work by joining the skull bones to different areas of skin, which are tugged as the muscles contract. The head is supported and moved by muscles that start at the backbone, shoulder blades, and bones in the upper chest.

Zygomatic muscles raise the corners of the mouth upward

Risorius pulls the corner of the mouth in a smile

Sternocleidomastoid tilts the head forward or to one side

Trapezius pulls the head upright

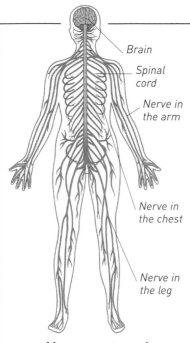

Brain
Spinal cord
Nerve in the arm
Nerve in the chest
Nerve in the leg

The nervous system

Without the control and coordination of its nervous system, the body could not function. With split-second timing, our nervous system allows us to feel, see, and hear, to move, and to think and remember—all at the same time. It also automatically controls many internal body processes. It is run by the brain and spinal cord, which form the central nervous system (CNS) and link to the body's network of nerves.

Nerve network

The brain and spinal cord form the control center of a network of nerves. Nerves are bundles of interconnected neuron cells and divide to reach all of the body's tissues. Laid end to end, a body's nerves would circle Earth twice.

Facial nerve controls the muscles of facial expression

Trigeminal nerve branch supplies the upper teeth and cheek

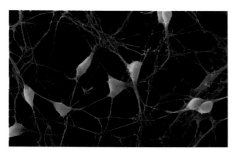

Pavlov's performing dogs

A reflex is an automatic reaction to a particular stimulus, or trigger. Dogs naturally salivate (drool) at the sight and smell of food. Russian scientist Ivan Pavlov (1849–1936) trained some dogs to associate feeding time with the sound of a bell. In time, they drooled when hearing the bell alone.

Cranial and spinal nerves

The brain—the cerebrum, cerebellum, and brain stem—and the spinal cord function through a constant flow of signals. These arrive and depart through 12 pairs of cranial nerves that start in the brain, and 31 pairs of spinal nerves that start in the spinal cord. Each nerve has sensory neurons, which carry sensations from a body area to the brain, and motor neurons, which carry instructions from the brain to move muscles in that same area. Part of the nervous system automatically controls vital processes that we are unaware of, such as the body's heart rate.

Brachial plexus leads to the nerves that supply the arm and hand

Ulnar nerve controls the muscles that bend the wrist and fingers

Intercostal nerve controls the muscles between the ribs

Branches everywhere

These are association neurons in the brain. Each has branching links with thousands of other neurons, forming a communication network with countless routes for nerve signals traveling beween neurons.

Cerebrum processes
and stores information

Cerebellum
controls
movement
and balance

Brain stem
controls the heart
rate and breathing

Spinal cord
relays signals
between the
spinal nerves
and the brain

Sympathetic
ganglion chain
controls automatic
functions

Spinal nerves
are arranged
in pairs

Phrenic nerve
supplies the
diaphragm,
the muscle that
causes breathing

Axon bundle
carries signals to
and from the brain

Spinal nerve

Front root carries
outgoing signals

Back root carries
incoming signals

Gray matter
contains
neuron cell
bodies

White matter
consists of
axon bundles

Meninges
are three
protective
membranes

Founder of neurology

French physician Jean-Martin
Charcot (1825–93) was a
pioneer of neurology, the study
of nervous system diseases,
and of psychiatry, the branch
of medicine that deals with
mental illness.

Cross-section of the spinal cord

The spinal cord relays nerve signals between
the spinal nerves and the brain. Each spinal
nerve has two roots. One contains sensory
neurons bringing incoming signals from sense
receptors. The other contains motor neurons
carrying outgoing signals to the muscles. The
spinal cord also controls many automatic body
reflexes, such as pulling the hand away from a
hot or sharp object.

Neuron structure

A neuron is a nerve cell body
with many short, branched
endings called dendrites and
one long axon, or nerve fiber.
Dendrites receive nerve signals
from other neurons across
junctions called synapses.
Axons carry nerve signals
away from the cell body,
across synapses with other
neurons or with muscles.

Part of
another
neuron

Neuron's cell
body contains
its nucleus

Synapse
between
two
neurons

Dendrite

Axon
(nerve fiber)

Longest axon
is up to 3 ft
(1 m) long

Insulating
myelin sheath
increases
speed of
signals

Vagus nerve
helps control
the heart rate

The brain

The brain is our most complex organ and our nervous system's control center. It contains 100 billion neurons (nerve cells), each linked to hundreds or thousands of other neurons, which together form a vast communication network with incredible processing power. Over the past two centuries, scientists have mapped the brain and how it works.

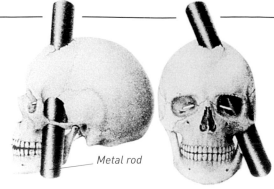

Metal rod

Hole in the head
Phineas Gage worked in a quarry in the US. In 1848, a gunpowder accident blew a metal rod through the left frontal lobe of his brain. Gage survived, but he changed from contented and polite to moody and foul-mouthed—living proof that the front of the brain is involved in personality.

The brain from below
The brain has three main parts. The cerebrum dominates the brain and makes up 85 percent of its weight. It processes and stores incoming information and sends out instructions to the body. The brain stem relays signals between the cerebrum and the spinal cord and controls automatic functions, such as the heart rate and breathing. The cerebellum is responsible for controlling balance and posture and for coordinating movements.

Left and right
The right hemisphere (half) of the cerebrum receives sensory input from and controls the movements of the left side of the body, and vice versa. The right side of the brain also handles face recognition and creative abilities such as music, while the left side controls language, problem solving, and mathematical skills. Left-handed people, such as rock guitarist Jimi Hendrix (1942–70), often excel in the creative arts and music.

Left hemisphere of cerebrum controls the right side of the body

Olfactory bulb carries signals from the nose to the brain

Optic nerve (shown cut) carries signals from the eyes to the brain

Pons is the middle part of the brain stem

Medulla oblongata is part of the brain stem that controls breathing and the heart rate

Cerebellum controls body movements

Right hemisphere of the cerebrum controls the left side of the body

Spinal cord (shown cut) relays signals between the brain and body

Premotor cortex controls complex movements

Primary motor cortex controls muscles

Primary sensory cortex receives input from skin

Sensory association cortex interprets touch signals

Visual association cortex interprets images

Prefrontal cortex controls reasoning and learning

Broca's area controls speech

Primary auditory cortex receives input from ears

Auditory association cortex interprets sounds

Primary visual cortex receives input from eyes

Wernicke's area interprets language

Brain map

Different areas of the cerebral cortex carry out specific tasks, as shown in this map of the left hemisphere. Sensory areas of the cortex deal with input from the sensory detectors. Motor areas of the cortex control the body's movement. Most of the cortex is made up of association areas that interpret and analyze information used in learning and memory.

Site of speech

French physician Paul Pierre Broca (1824–80) had a patient with a limited ability to speak. After the patient died, Broca found a damaged patch on his left cerebrum. He realized this area coordinated the muscles of the larynx and mouth that are used for speaking.

Frontal lobe at the front of the cerebral hemisphere

Left cerebral hemisphere

Temporal lobe at the side of the cerebral hemisphere

Parietal lobe on the rear top section of the cerebral hemisphere

Occipital lobe at the back of the cerebral hemisphere

Longitudinal fissure separates the two cerebral hemispheres

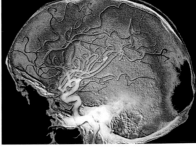

Blood supply

This angiogram shows the brain's blood supply. The brain makes up only two percent of the body's weight, but receives 20 percent of the body's total blood supply. This delivers the oxygen and glucose (sugar) that the brain requires to function normally.

Gyrus (ridge)

Right cerebral hemisphere

Sulcus (groove)

The brain from above

The surface layer of the cerebrum, called the cerebral cortex, is heavily folded with ridges and grooves. These greatly increase the surface area of cerebral cortex that can fit inside the skull. If laid out flat, the cortex would cover about the same area as a pillow. Deep grooves divide each hemisphere into four areas, called the frontal, temporal, parietal, and occipital lobes.

Inside the brain

Deep inside the brain, under the cerebrum, the thalamus acts as a relay station for incoming nerve signals, and the hypothalamus automatically controls a vast array of body activities. The limbic system is the emotional center of the brain, dealing with instincts, fears, and feelings. Inside the cerebrum, linked chambers called ventricles are filled with cerebrospinal fluid (CSF). CSF is produced by blood and circulates through the ventricles, helping to feed the brain cells.

Liquid brainpower
Long ago, a mystical animal spirit was said to fill the brain's ventricles. This 17th-century image links each ventricle to a different mental quality, such as imagination.

Matters of the mind
Austrian physician Sigmund Freud (1856–1939) used psychoanalysis to treat mental illness by investigating the unconscious mind. Since Freud, psychiatrists have linked mental disorders to abnormalities in the brain's structure and its biochemical workings.

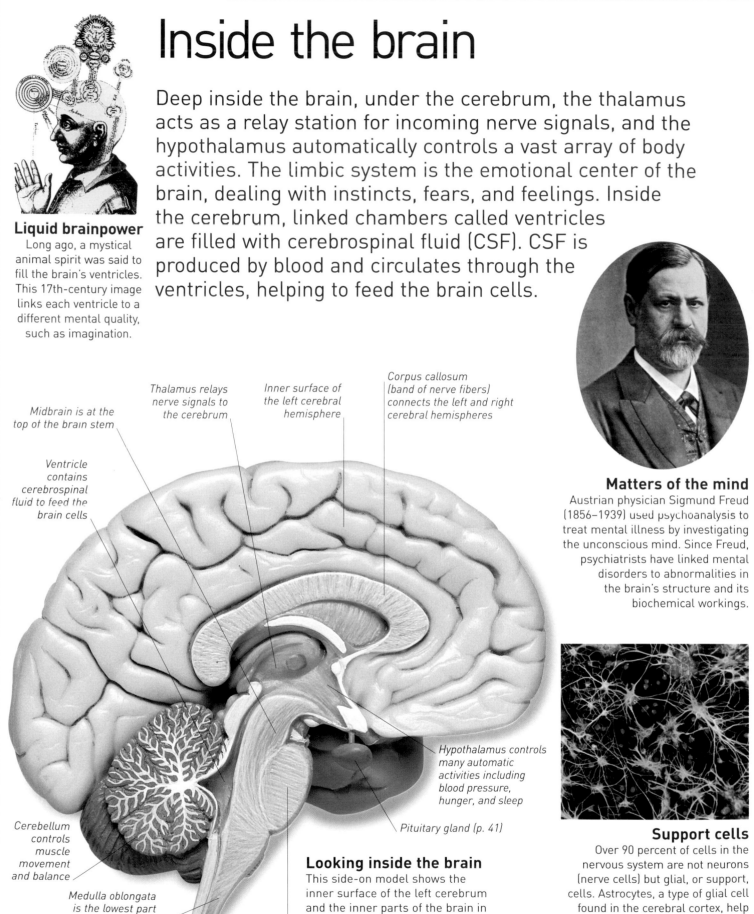

Midbrain is at the top of the brain stem

Thalamus relays nerve signals to the cerebrum

Inner surface of the left cerebral hemisphere

Corpus callosum (band of nerve fibers) connects the left and right cerebral hemispheres

Ventricle contains cerebrospinal fluid to feed the brain cells

Hypothalamus controls many automatic activities including blood pressure, hunger, and sleep

Cerebellum controls muscle movement and balance

Pituitary gland (p. 41)

Medulla oblongata is the lowest part of the brain stem

Pons is in the middle of the brain stem

Spinal cord (shown cut)

Looking inside the brain
This side-on model shows the inner surface of the left cerebrum and the inner parts of the brain in cross-section. The thalamus sits in the center of the brain. The cerebellum is at the back of the brain, behind the brain stem.

Support cells
Over 90 percent of cells in the nervous system are not neurons (nerve cells) but glial, or support, cells. Astrocytes, a type of glial cell found in the cerebral cortex, help to supply neurons with nutrients. Other functions of glial cells include destroying bacteria and insulating axons (nerve fibers).

The limbic system

A curve of linked structures is located on the inner surface of each cerebral hemisphere and around the top of the brain stem. It deals with emotions such as pleasure, anger, fear, hope, and sadness, and helps us to store memories. Because the sense of smell is linked to the limbic system, certain odors can trigger feelings and memories.

Cingulate gyrus deals with emotions

Fornix is the pathway that links different parts of the limbic system

Olfactory bulb carries signals from the smell receptors in the nose directly to the limbic system

Mamillary body relays signals from the amygdala and hippocampus to the thalamus

Hippocampus deals with memory and navigation

Parahippocampal gyrus deals with anger and fright, and recalls memories

Amygdala assesses danger and triggers feelings of fear

Deep thought

French sculptor Auguste Rodin (1840–1917) portrayed deep concentration in his statue *The Thinker*. When we want to think hard about a matter, we stare into space, almost unseeing, so that we can concentrate.

Sweet dreams

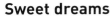

French artist Henri Rousseau (1844–1910) painted a musician dreaming about a lion in *The Sleeping Gypsy*. In our dreams, real experiences can be mixed up with strange happenings. While we sleep, the brain replays recent experiences at random and stores significant events in the memory. Dreaming is a side effect of this activity.

White matter of cerebrum consists of axons encased in insulating sheaths

Cerebral cortex consists of gray matter

Longitudinal fissure separates the left and right cerebral hemispheres

Fornix is the nerve pathway that links parts of the limbic system

Corpus callosum (band of nerve fibers)

Basal nuclei are deep areas of gray matter that control body movement

Thalamus relays incoming signals to the cerebral cortex

Ventricle

Gray and white matter

This vertical cross-section gives a front view of the parts of the cerebrum. The cerebral cortex—the surface layer of the brain—is made up of gray matter. This consists of neuron cell bodies, dendrites, and short axons. White matter consists of longer axons, which join parts of the cerebral cortex together, or connect the brain to the rest of the nervous system.

Pons

Cerebellum

Spinal cord

Medulla oblongata

Mind over matter

Scientists continue to explore how the brain works. Some people look beyond its nerve signals and chemical processes, and believe that techniques such as meditation, performed here by a Buddhist monk, can carry the mind beyond the physical boundaries of the body.

Skin and touch

In addition to its role in the sense of touch, skin has many other jobs. Its tough surface layer, the epidermis, keeps out water, dust, germs, and harmful ultraviolet rays from the Sun. Underneath is a thicker layer, the dermis, which is packed with sensory receptors, nerves, and blood vessels. It helps steady our body temperature at 98.6°F (37°C) by releasing sweat. Hair and nails provide additional body covering and protection.

Cooling the body

This is one of about three million sweat pores in the skin's surface. When sweat glands in the dermis release sweat through the pores, the process draws heat from the body and cools it down.

Fingertip reading

The Braille system enables people with sight problems to read using the sense of touch. It uses patterns of raised dots to represent letters and numbers, which are felt through the sensitive fingertips. The system was devised in 1824 by French teenager Louis Braille (1809–52), who was blinded at three years old.

Under your skin

The upper surface of the epidermis consists of dead cells filled with a tough protein, keratin. The skin flakes as dead cells wear away and are replaced with new ones produced in the lowest layer of the epidermis. The thicker dermis layer contains the sense receptors that help the body detect changes in temperature, touch, vibration, pressure, and pain. The dermis also houses coiled sweat glands and hair follicles. Oily sebum keeps the skin and hair soft and flexible.

Ridges on fingertips aid grip (see opposite)

Lines on the palm of the hand

Get a grip

The skin on the palm of the hand is covered with ridges. These help the hand to grip objects when performing different tasks. Beneath the palm, a triangle-shaped sheet of tough, meshed fibers anchors the skin and stops it from sliding over the underlying fat and muscle.

Light touch and pressure receptor

Lowest layer of the epidermis replaces surface cells

Sebaceous gland releases sebum through the hair follicle

Temperature or pain receptor

Hair

Epidermis consists of several layers

Sweat pore

Upper layer of the epidermis

Nerve carries signals to the brain

Sweat gland

Fingerprints

The skin on the fingers, toes, palms, and soles is folded into swirling patterns of tiny ridges. The ridges help this skin to grip, aided by sweat released through pores along each ridge. When fingers touch smooth surfaces, such as glass, their ridges leave behind sweaty patterns, or prints, featuring arches, loops, and whorls. Each human has a unique set of fingerprints.

Loop pattern on fingerprint

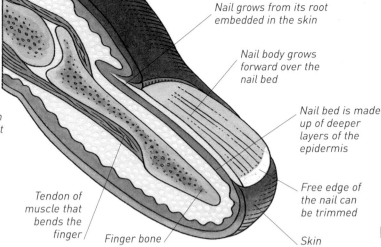

Nail grows from its root embedded in the skin

Nail body grows forward over the nail bed

Nail bed is made up of deeper layers of the epidermis

Free edge of the nail can be trimmed

Skin

Tendon of muscle that bends the finger

Finger bone

Insensitive nails

Nails protect the ends of fingers and toes. They are hard extensions of the epidermis, made from dead cells filled with keratin. Each nail grows from new cells produced in the root. These push the nail body forward over the nail bed as it grows.

Uncut fingernails curl as they grow

Nail growth

A typical fingernail grows about 1/8 in (3 mm) in a month. The nails on the longer fingers grow faster than those on the shorter ones. Fingernails also grow faster in the summer months than in winter. Toenails grow three or four times more slowly.

Hair follicle contains the growing hair

Light touch receptor

Blood vessels supply the skin cells

Fingertips are packed with touch receptors

Tongue and lips are very sensitive

Face has sensitive areas

A sensitive body

Different parts of the body have varying numbers of sense receptors in the skin for detecting touch, pressure, and vibration. This body is exaggerated to show which areas of skin have the most, and are therefore most sensitive to touch.

Back of knee is not very sensitive

Dermis is firmly attached to the epidermis

Pressure and vibration receptor

Fat layer under the dermis insulates the body

Dead hairs

These hair shafts in the skin grow from living cells at the base of the follicle. As the cells push upward, they fill with keratin and die. Short, fine hairs cover much of the body. Longer, thicker hairs protect the scalp from harmful sunlight and prevent heat loss.

Skin color

Skin color depends on how much melanin, or brown pigment (coloring), it contains. Melanin is produced by cells in the lowest layer of the epidermis. It protects against the harmful, ultraviolet rays in sunlight, which can damage skin cells and the tissues underneath. Sudden exposure of pale skin to strong sunlight can produce sunburn.

Eyes and seeing

The eyes contain over 70 percent of the body's sensory receptors, in the form of light-detecting cells. Our eyes move automatically, adjust to dim and bright light, and focus light from objects near or far. This light is turned into electrical signals, sent to the brain, and changed into the images we see.

Cross-eyed
This Arabic drawing, nearly 1,000 years old, shows how the optic nerves cross. Half of the nerve fibers from the right eye pass to the left side of the brain, and vice versa.

Outer layers
The wall of the eyeball has three layers. Outermost is the tough sclera, visible at the front as the white of the eye, except where the clear cornea allows light in. Next is the choroid, filled with blood vessels that supply the other two layers. The innermost layer is the retina. Millions of light-detecting cells at the back of the retina send image information to the brain.

Medial rectus turns the eye inward toward the nose

Superior rectus moves the eye upward

Superior oblique muscle rotates the eye downward and outward, away from the nose

Lateral rectus moves the eye outward

Inferior oblique rotates the eye upward and outward

Inferior rectus moves the eye downward

Moving the eye
Eyeballs automatically swivel in their sockets to follow moving objects. They also make tiny, jumping movements when scanning a face or the words on this page. Just six slim muscles produce all these movements.

Suspensory ligament

Fovea

Pupil is the hole in the center of the iris

Cornea

Lens

Iris

Ciliary muscles

Sclera

Eyelids and tears
Soft, flexible eyelids protect the eyes and wash them with tears at each blink. Tears are produced by a lacrimal (tear) gland behind each upper eyelid and flow along tiny ducts (tubes) to be spread over the eye with each blink. Tears keep the eye moist and wash away dust and other irritants. Used tear fluid drains away through two tiny holes in the eyelids near the nose and along two ducts into the nose. That's why crying hard produces a runny nose, too.

Eyes forward

Only one-sixth of an eyeball can be seen from the outside. The rest sits protected within a deep bowl of skull bone, the eye socket. Eyebrows, eyelids, and eyelashes protect the front of the eye by shading it from dust, sweat, and excessive light. The color of the iris depends on the amount of the brown pigment melanin present.

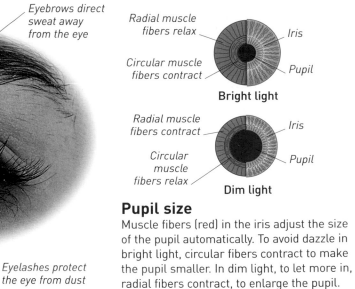

Eyelids protect the eye from bright light

Eyebrows direct sweat away from the eye

Radial muscle fibers relax — Iris

Circular muscle fibers contract — Pupil

Bright light

Radial muscle fibers contract — Iris

Circular muscle fibers relax — Pupil

Dim light

Tears drain away through two ducts in the corner of the eye

Pupil lets light into the eye

Eyelashes protect the eye from dust

Pupil size

Muscle fibers (red) in the iris adjust the size of the pupil automatically. To avoid dazzle in bright light, circular fibers contract to make the pupil smaller. In dim light, to let more in, radial fibers contract, to enlarge the pupil.

Vitreous humor within the body of the eyeball

Blind spot is the area that lacks rods and cones

Optic nerve carries nerve signals from the retina to the brain

Retina

Choroid

Forming an image

When we look at an object, light rays reflected from that object are partly focused, or bent, by the cornea. The light then passes through the pupil to the lens, which projects a sharp upside-down image onto the retina. It sends nerve signals along the optic nerve to the brain, which turns the image the right way up.

Partial focus by the cornea

Fine-tune focus by the lens

Upside-down image formed at the back of the retina

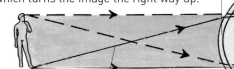

Light rays from the object transmitted to the eye

Lens shape is adjusted by the ciliary muscles

Optic nerve

Rods and cones

The retina has two kinds of light-detecting cell. The rods (green) see only in shades of gray, but respond well in dim light. The cones (blue) are mainly at the back of the retina and see details and colors, but work well only in bright light.

Inside the eye

Behind the cornea, the iris controls the amount of light entering the eye through the pupil. The space behind the lens is filled with clear, jellylike vitreous humor. The most detailed images are produced where light falls on the fovea, a part of the retina that contains only cones (see above, right).

Eye advances

German scientist Hermann von Helmholtz (1821–94) studied the mathematics of the eye in the *Handbook of Physiological Optics*. He also helped to invent the ophthalmoscope. Doctors use this light-and-lens device for close-up examinations of the eye's interior.

Ears and hearing

After sight, hearing provides the brain with the most information about the outside world. It enables us to figure out the source, direction, and nature of sounds, and to communicate with each other. Our ears detect waves of pressure, called sound waves, which travel through the air from a vibrating sound source. The ears turn these waves into nerve signals, which the brain interprets as sounds that range from loud to quiet and from high pitched to low.

The mind's ear
German composer and pianist Ludwig van Beethoven (1770–1827) went deaf but continued to compose masterpieces by imagining the notes in his head.

Ear pioneer
The Examination of the Organ of Hearing, published in 1562, was probably the first major work devoted to ears. Its author was the Italian Bartolomeo Eustachio (c. 1520–74), a professor of anatomy in Rome. His name lives on in the Eustachian tube that he discovered, which connects the middle ear to the back of the throat.

Temporal bone of the skull

Scalp muscle

Cartilage supporting the pinna

The eardrum
The eardrum is a taut, delicate membrane, like the stretched skin on a drum, that vibrates when sound waves enter the ear. It separates the outer ear from the middle ear. Doctors can examine the eardrum through a medical instrument called an otoscope.

Hammer is one of three tiny bones behind the semitransparent eardrum

Outer ear canal

Why ears pop
With equal air pressure on either side of the eardrum, it vibrates freely and so we hear clearly. A sudden change in pressure disrupts this. Yawning or swallowing opens the Eustachian tube and causes the ears to pop, as air moves into the middle ear and restores equal pressures.

Eustachian tube links the middle ear and throat

18th-century drawing of the ear

Inside the ear
Most of the ear lies inside the skull's temporal bone. It has three main parts. In the outer ear, the pinna (ear flap) directs sound waves into the ear canal. In the air-filled middle ear, behind the eardrum, three tiny bones called ossicles convert the sound waves into mechanical movement. The fluid-filled inner ear converts that movement into nerve signals.

Ear lobe of the pinna (ear flap)

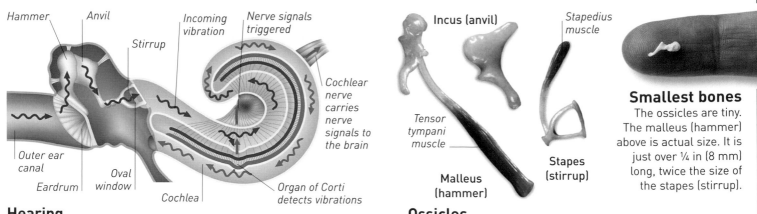

Hammer · Anvil · Stirrup · Incoming vibration · Nerve signals triggered · Cochlear nerve carries nerve signals to the brain · Outer ear canal · Eardrum · Oval window · Cochlea · Organ of Corti detects vibrations

Incus (anvil) · Stapedius muscle · Tensor tympani muscle · Malleus (hammer) · Stapes (stirrup)

Smallest bones

The ossicles are tiny. The malleus (hammer) above is actual size. It is just over ¼ in (8 mm) long, twice the size of the stapes (stirrup).

Hearing

Sound waves funnelled into the ear canal strike the eardrum, making it vibrate. This makes the three ossicles move back and forth. The stirrup pushes and pulls the flexible oval window like a piston. This sets up vibrations in the fluid filling the cochlea. Inside the cochlea, sound-detecting hair cells turn the vibrations into nerve signals. These pass along the cochlear nerve to the hearing area of the brain.

Ossicles

The ossicles are the smallest bones in the body. They get their Latin names from their shapes. Attached to the bones are two of the body's smallest muscles. If a very loud sound reaches the eardrum, they contract to reduce the intense vibrations that would damage the inner ear.

The inner ear

The innermost part of the ear is made up of a maze of channels filled with fluid. One branch leads to the coiled cochlea. The vestibule houses the oval window—the membrane between the middle and inner ears—and two organs of balance, the utricle and saccule. Above the vestibule lies another balance organ, the semicircular canals.

Middle ear links the inner and outer ears · Semicircular canals · Vestibular nerve carries signals from the balance organs to the brain · Cochlea · Cochlear nerve carries signals from the cochlea to the brain · Vestibule contains the utricle and saccule balance organs · Eardrum divides the outer ear from the middle ear · Oval window · Ossicles (ear bones) link the eardrum to the oval window · Eustachian tube

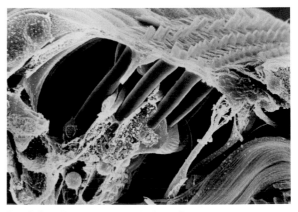

Inside the organ of Corti

When sound vibrations pass through the cochlea's fluid, hair cells (red) move up and down. This squashes them, causing hair cells to send signals to the brain. They do the same in the balance organs.

Balancing act

The inner ear houses the fluid-filled organs that help the body stay balanced. The three semicircular canals detect the rotation of the head in any direction. The utricle and saccule detect when the head—and body—accelerates. These balance organs constantly update the brain, so that it can keep the body upright.

Smell and taste

The senses of smell and taste are closely linked—both detect chemicals. Taste receptors on the tongue detect substances in drink and food. Olfactory (smell) receptors in the nasal cavity pick up odor molecules in air. The two senses enable us to detect all kinds of scents and flavors, good and bad.

Bad air
For centuries, physicians thought diseases were carried by foul-smelling air. This 14th-century physician holds aromatic herbs to his nose to avoid catching his patient's illness.

Left cerebral hemisphere of the brain

Skull bone

Olfactory bulb carries the smell signals to the front of the brain

Branching olfactory nerves connect to the olfactory bulb

Nasal conchae (shelves of bone covered in nasal lining) keep the air inside the nose moist

Nasal cavity connects the nostrils to the throat

Mouth cavity

Tongue surface is covered with papillae, bearing taste buds

Chorda tympani branch of the facial nerve carries taste signals from the front two-thirds of the tongue

One of the muscles that moves the tongue

Neuron (nerve cell) carries signals to the brain

Olfactory bulb

Axon of olfactory nerve passes through a channel in the skull bone

Smell receptor cell

Cilia of receptor cell

Odor molecules

Cross-section inside the nose
The nasal cavity's lining (pink) contains thousands of smell receptor cells The cells' hairlike cilia project into the watery mucus of the nasal lining. They detect odor molecules in the air and relay signals to the olfactory nerve, the olfactory bulb, and the brain.

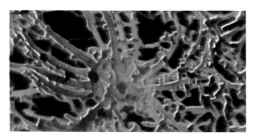

Odor detectors
Odor molecules dissolve in mucus and bind to these cilia, triggering the receptor cells to send signals to the brain. Olfactory receptors can distinguish between 10,000 smells.

Smell and taste pathways
A cross-section through the head shows the routes taken by nerve signals from smell receptors in the nose, and from taste buds in the tongue. In the nasal cavity, branches of the olfactory nerve send signals to the olfactory bulb, which carries the signals to the areas at the front of the brain that identify smells. Taste signals from the front and back of the tongue travel along separate nerves to the brain stem's medulla oblongata. From here they are sent to the area of the brain where tastes are recognized.

Vallate papillae
detect bitter tastes

Filiform papillae
detect temperature
and texture

Vagus nerve carries
signals from taste
buds in the throat

Nerve carries
taste signals
from the back
of the tongue

Lingual
nerve
carries
touch
signals
from the
front of
the tongue

Facial nerve
carries taste
signals from the
front of the tongue

Fungiform
papillae
detect four
different
tastes

Taste organ

The muscular tongue
mixes and tastes food
during chewing. It is
covered with pimplelike
papillae of different types. These
make the tongue sensitive to taste
and also to touch and temperature.

Gustatory
(taste) area on
the left side of
the brain

Pons (part of the brain
stem) carries signals
from the medulla
oblongata to the brain

Medulla oblongata
(part of the brain
stem) receives signals
from the facial and
glossopharyngeal nerves

Spinal cord

Glossopharyngeal
nerve carries taste
signals from the rear
one-third of the tongue

Throat

Taste
receptor cell

Taste pore

Taste hair

Supporting
cell

Nerve fiber
carries taste
signals to
the brain

Tongue
skin cell

Taste buds

There are around 10,000 taste buds on the tongue,
located on certain papillae. Taste molecules
dissolve in saliva during chewing and pass into a
taste bud through a pore. The hairs at the top of the
taste receptor cells detect one of five tastes—
sweet, sour, salty, bitter, or umami (savory).

Papillae and taste buds

This SEM shows two types of
papillae at the tip of the tongue.
The larger, mushroom-shaped
fungiform papillae contain taste
buds. Spiked filiform papillae give
the tongue its rough surface for
gripping food during chewing,
and their receptors detect the
texture and temperature of food.

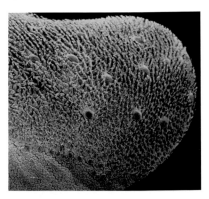

Hormones

A second control system works alongside the brain and nerve network. The endocrine system is a collection of glands that release chemical messengers, or hormones, into the bloodstream. They control body processes, such as growth and reproduction, by targeting specific body cells and altering their chemical activities. Located in the brain, the hypothalamus links the two control systems.

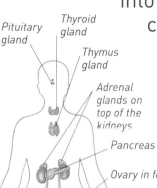

Pituitary gland
Thyroid gland
Thymus gland
Adrenal glands on top of the kidneys
Pancreas
Ovary in female
Testis in male

Hypothalamus

Nerve cells in the front of the hypothalamus produce the hormones oxytocin and ADH

Pituitary stalk connects the hypothalamus to the pituitary gland

Blood vessels carry regulating hormones from the hypothalamus to the front of the pituitary gland

Front lobe of the pituitary gland is stimulated to release its hormones by regulating hormones from the hypothalamus

Endocrine system

The glands that make up the endocrine system lie inside the head and torso. Some endocrine glands, such as the thyroid, are organs in their own right. Other glands are embedded in an organ that also has other functions.

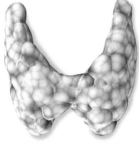

Thyroid gland

This gland makes two main hormones. Thyroxine targets most body cells and increases their metabolism (chemical processes) to stimulate growth and development. Calcitonin triggers the bones' uptake of calcium from blood.

Right kidney

Adrenal gland

Adrenal glands

The two adrenal glands on the kidneys produce corticosteroids, hormones that regulate the levels of salt and water in the blood, speed up the body's metabolism, and deal with stress. The medulla inside each kidney releases epinephrine, the hormone that prepares the body to deal with threats (see left).

Fight or flight

The hormone epinephrine prepares the body to fight or flee in the face of danger. It does this by rapidly boosting heart and breathing rates and diverting blood and extra glucose (sugar) to the muscles.

Vein carries hormones to the body

Hypothalamus

The almond-sized hypothalamus at the base of the brain controls a range of body activities, sometimes through the pituitary gland. Nerve cells in the rear of the hypothalamus produce regulating hormones that travel in the bloodstream to the front lobe of the pituitary, to stimulate the release of pituitary hormones. Nerve cells in the front of the hypothalamus make two more hormones that nerve fibers carry to the rear of the pituitary.

Nerve cells in the rear of the hypothalamus release regulating hormones into the blood vessels supplying the front lobe

Pancreas

The pancreas has two roles. Most of its tissues are gland cells that make digestive enzymes for release along ducts into the small intestine. The endocrine tissues release the hormones insulin and glucagon directly into the bloodstream. These two hormones maintain steady levels of glucose—the sugar removed from food to fuel the body—in the blood.

Nerve fibers carry oxytocin and ADH to the rear lobe of the pituitary gland

Artery (cut) carries fresh blood to the pituitary

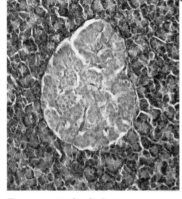

Pancreatic islets

The tissue inside the pancreas is dotted with more than one million clusters of cells called islets of Langerhans (center). In the 1890s, scientists discovered the cells released secretions, later called hormones.

**Sir Frederick Banting
(1891–1941)**

**Charles Best
(1899–1978)**

The insulin story

A lack of the hormone insulin in the body causes a serious condition called diabetes, where blood glucose levels soar. In 1922, Canadian Frederick Banting and American Charles Best successfully extracted insulin so that it could be used to treat and control this disorder.

Rear lobe of the pituitary gland stores and releases ADH and oxytocin

Pituitary gland

The pea-sized pituitary gland is attached to the base of the brain and has separate front and rear parts, or lobes. Front lobe cells make six hormones that affect metabolism, growth, and reproduction, usually by triggering another gland to release hormones. The rear lobe stores and releases antidiuretic hormone (ADH), which controls urine's water levels, and oxytocin, which makes the uterus contract during labor.

Thymus gland

The thymus gland is large in childhood but shrinks in adult life. During a child's early years, it produces two hormones that ensure the normal development of white blood cells called T cells, or T lymphocytes. These identify and destroy disease-causing organisms, such as bacteria. This SEM shows undeveloped T cells (yellow) in the thymus gland.

The heart

Organ storage
In Egyptians mummies, most body organs were removed and stored in jars such as these. The heart was left in place, ready for the afterlife.

The ancient Egyptians believed the heart housed the soul. For the Greeks it was the seat of love and intelligence. In fact, it is an extraordinarily reliable, muscular pump, with a separate right and left side. Each side has two linked chambers—an upper, thin-walled atrium and a larger, thick-walled ventricle below. The right ventricle pumps oxygen-poor blood to the lungs to pick up oxygen and then back to the left atrium. The left ventricle pumps oxygen-rich blood around the body and back to the right atrium. To do this, the heart beats some billion times in an average lifetime.

The right connections
Italian anatomist Andrea Cesalpino (1519 1603) realized how the heart connects to the main blood vessels and the lungs, but not how the circulatory system works (p. 44).

Right coronary artery

Aorta

Left coronary artery

Coronary vein

Coronary sinus (main coronary vein)

Small connecting blood vessels

Main branch of the left coronary artery

Valve open

Valve closed

Blood flows away from the heart

Blood pushes through the open valve as the heart contracts

Blood flows back and shuts the valve as the heart relaxes

Blood is pumped out of the heart

Valves at work
Valves ensure the one-way flow of blood. The aortic and pulmonary valves at the two exits from the heart have pocket-shaped flaps of tissue. When the heart contracts, blood pushes its way out, pressing the flaps open. When the heart relaxes, blood tries to flow back, pressing the flaps shut.

Coronary circulation
The heart's muscular wall has its own blood supply—the coronary circulation—that delivers oxygen to keep the heart beating. Left and right coronary arteries stem from the aorta and branch out to carry oxygen-rich blood to the heart wall. Oxygen-poor blood is taken by coronary veins to the coronary sinus. This large vein at the back of the heart empties blood into the right atrium, ready to go around the heart again.

Heart rate
The average adult heart beats 60–80 times a minute, pumping up to 11 pints (6 liters) of blood per minute. Each beat creates a pressure surge through the body's arteries. This pulse can be felt in the artery in the wrist. During activity, the muscles need more oxygen and nutrients, so the heart beats faster and harder—up to 150 times a minute in the fittest individuals.

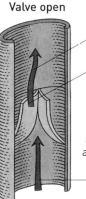

Brachiocephalic artery to the right side of the head and brain, and right arm

Superior vena cava brings oxygen-poor blood from the head and upper body

Left common carotid artery to the left side of the head and brain

Left subclavian artery to the left arm

Aorta

Right atrium

Pulmonary artery takes oxygen-poor blood to the lungs

Left atrium

Left pulmonary veins bring oxygen-rich blood from the left lung

Pulmonary valve

Aortic valve

Bicuspid valve

Thick muscular wall of left ventricle

Left ventricle

Right pulmonary veins bring oxygen-rich blood from the right lung

Tricuspid valve

Right ventricle

Right ventricle wall is thinner than the left

Inferior vena cava brings oxygen-poor blood from the abdomen and legs

Descending aorta takes oxygen-rich blood to the lower body and legs

Septum separates the left and right sides of the heart

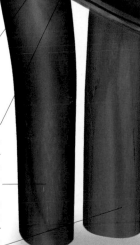

How the heart beats

Natural pacemaker cells in the right atrium wall produce electrical signals to maintain a regular heartbeat. With each beat, the left side of the heart takes in oxygen-rich blood from the lungs and pumps it around the body, while the right side receives oxygen-poor blood from the body and pumps it to the lungs to pick up oxygen.

Blood enters from the body

Blood enters from the lungs

Muscular walls relax

1 Relax and refill

When the cardiac muscle relaxes, blood flows in under low pressure to the right atrium from the body, and to the left atrium from the lungs.

Atrial walls contract

Bicuspid valve opens

Tricuspid valve opens

2 Atria contract

An electrical signal from the pacemaker cells causes the atria to contract. This pumps blood into the ventricles, through their tricuspid and bicuspid valves.

Blood out to the body

Blood out to the lungs

Pulmonary valve opens

Aortic valve opens

Tricuspid valve closes

Bicuspid valve closes

Ventricle walls contract

3 Ventricles contract

The electrical signal passes through the ventricle walls, so they contract. Blood is forced into the aorta and pulmonary artery, and the ventricles valves snap shut—producing the heartbeat you hear.

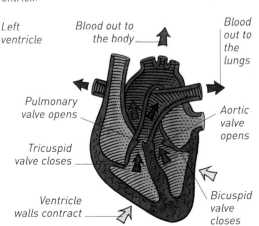

Inside the heart

This cutaway reveals the atria and ventricles. The muscular ventricle walls contract to pump blood out of the heart. The wall of the left ventricle, which pumps blood to the whole body, is thicker than that of the right, which pumps blood a shorter distance to the lungs. In just one day, the ventricles pump up to 3,300 gallons (15,000 liters) of blood.

In circulation

The body's trillions of cells need a constant supply of oxygen, nutrients, and other essentials, and the constant removal of wastes. The heart pumps blood around the body, delivering essentials to cells through a vast network of blood vessels. A second transportation system, called the lymphatic system, drains excess fluid from the tissues. The two systems also play key parts in fighting disease.

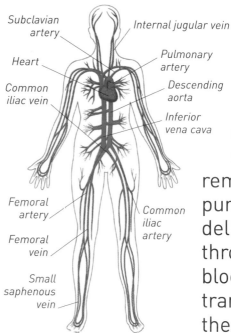

Subclavian artery
Internal jugular vein
Heart
Pulmonary artery
Common iliac vein
Descending aorta
Inferior vena cava
Femoral artery
Common iliac artery
Femoral vein
Small saphenous vein

Circulatory system

Arteries carry oxygen-rich blood from the heart to body tissues, and veins return oxygen-poor blood from the tissues to the heart. Capillaries, too small to be seen here, carry blood through the tissues and connect arteries to veins.

Around and around

Until the 17th century, blood was thought to flow backward and forward inside arteries and veins. Experiments by English physician William Harvey (1578–1657) showed how the heart pumped blood around the body in one direction.

William Harvey, with King Charles I (seated)

Vein valves

Harvey based his theory of blood circulation on careful study, not tradition. His approach marked the beginning of scientific medicine. Harvey's illustrations show how the blood in veins always flows toward the heart. Valves, here marked by letters, prevent it from seeping backward.

Blood vessels of the leg

The external iliac artery carries oxygen-rich blood from the heart to the leg. Here it divides into branches that then subdivide to form the microscopic capillaries that deliver oxygen and nutrients to cells, and remove their waste products. The capillaries then rejoin, forming larger vessels that connect into the network of major veins that carry oxygen-poor blood from the leg back toward the heart.

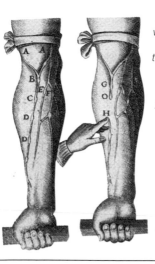

Small saphenous vein carries blood from the foot and lower leg

Small posterior tibial arteries supply blood to the foot and lower leg

External iliac artery
External iliac vein
Pelvis (hip bone)
Femoral vein carries blood from the thigh
Branch of femoral artery supplies blood to the thigh
Great saphenous vein carries blood from the foot and leg

Vessel investigator

Swiss-born anatomist Albrecht von Haller (1708–77) investigated how muscle in the wall of smaller arteries could contract or relax to vary the amount of blood flowing to a particular body part.

Blood vessels

With every heartbeat, an artery's walls expand and shrink as blood from the heart surges through it at high pressure. Veins carry blood returning from capillaries at low pressure, so their wall layers are thinner and less muscular. Just one cell thick, capillary walls let food and oxygen pass from blood into the surrounding tissues.

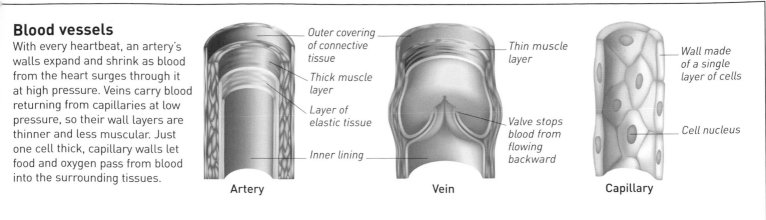

Artery
- Outer covering of connective tissue
- Thick muscle layer
- Layer of elastic tissue
- Inner lining

Vein
- Thin muscle layer
- Valve stops blood from flowing backward

Capillary
- Wall made of a single layer of cells
- Cell nucleus

Fighting infection

Every day, the body is exposed to pathogens—microscopic organisms, such as bacteria and viruses, that cause disease if they invade the body's tissues and bloodstream. White blood cells in the circulatory and lymphatic systems form the body's immune, or defense, system. Some patrol the body and search for invaders to destroy. Others attack specific pathogens and retain a memory of them, in case the same pathogens return to infect the body.

- Thymus gland processes lymphocytes
- Lymph vessels drain lymph from the tissues
- Lymph empties into the blood at the subclavian artery
- Thoracic duct
- Spleen produces large numbers of lymphocytes
- Lymph nodes clustered around the groin

Lymphatic system

This network of vessels drains excess fluid from the body's tissues and returns it to the bloodstream. The lymphatic system has no pump; instead the contractions of skeletal muscles push the fluid, called lymph, along the lymph vessels. As it flows, lymph passes through small swellings called lymph nodes.

Immune system

The macrophages and lymphocytes—white blood cells also called T and B cells—of the immune system respond to the invasion of pathogens by detecting and destroying them.

Macrophage

Shigella bacterium

1 Capturing a pathogen

Macrophages are white blood cells that hunt for pathogens in the body's tissues. This one has captured a bacterium called *Shigella* and will eat it up.

Antigens (remains of the destroyed bacterium)

2 Recognizing antigens

The macrophage displays antigens, or the remains of the bacterium, on its surface, to activate a helper T cell.

Antibodies attach themselves to a Shigella bacterium

5 Disabling the pathogen

Antibodies bind to the antigens on the *Shigella* bacterium's surface. This tags it for macrophages or other white blood cells to destroy.

Helper T cell

Antibody

B cell

4 Making antibodies

Plasma cells release billions of antibody molecules into the blood and lymph. The antibodies track down any *Shigella* bacteria present in the body.

3 Spurred into action

The helper T cell releases substances that switch on a B cell that targets *Shigella*. The B cell multiplies to produce plasma cells.

Plasma cell

The blood

Feeding on blood
Leeches and vampire bats feed on the blood of other animals. This scene from the 1978 film *Nosferatu* shows a mythical human vampire feeding on blood to gain immortality.

Red blood cell has no nucleus and a dimpled shape

An average adult has 9 pints (5 liters) of blood coursing around the body. Each drop of blood consists of millions of cells floating in liquid plasma. Red blood cells deliver essential oxygen to the body's tissues, while defense cells fight off infections. Blood also distributes heat to keep the body at a steady 98.6°F (37°C)—the ideal temperature for cells to function.

Blood transfusions
Before the discovery of blood groups, the transfusion (transfer) of blood from a donor—usually a healthy person, but here a dog—to a sick patient, often failed, killing the patient.

Red and white blood cells

Each type of blood cell has a vital role to play in the body. Red blood cells, by far the most numerous, transport oxygen to body cells. White blood cells, including neutrophils and lymphocytes help to defend the body against pathogens, or disease-causing germs. Neutrophils track down pathogens such as disease-causing bacteria, and then eat them. Lymphocytes are part of the immune system that targets and destroys specific germs. Platelets help to seal wounds by forming blood clots.

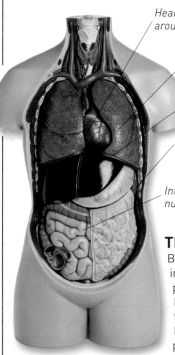

Heart pumps blood around the body

Lungs transfer oxygen and carbon dioxide to and from the blood

Liver controls the concentration of many chemicals in the blood

Spleen removes old, worn-out red blood cells and helps recycle their iron

Intestines transfer digested nutrients from food into the blood

Three main roles

Blood transports a range of substances, including oxygen, nutrients, and waste products from cells. It also protects the body by carrying white blood cells and forming blood clots. And it controls body temperature by distributing heat produced by organs around the body.

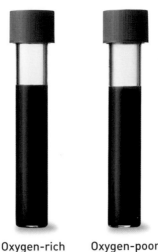

Plasma makes up 55% of blood

White blood cells and platelets make up 1% of blood

Red blood cells make up 44% of blood

Settled blood　　**Oxygen-rich blood**　　**Oxygen-poor blood**

Neutrophil has a nucleus consisting of many lobes

Blood components

If allowed to settle, blood separates into three parts. The red and white blood cells float in a yellow liquid called plasma. This is mainly water containing over 100 substances including oxygen, nutrients, blood proteins, hormones, and wastes.

Changing color

Blood takes its color from the red blood cells. When they pick up oxygen in the lungs, blood turns bright red. Once they unload oxygen in the tissues, blood turns a darker shade of red.

Blood groups

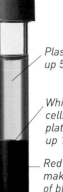

Austrian-American scientist Karl Landsteiner (1868–1943) found that people belonged to one of four blood groups: A, B, AB, or O. Doctors can match blood types to keep a body from rejecting a blood transfusion from the wrong blood group.

Lymphocyte has a nucleus that fills most of the cell

Platelet is a cell fragment rather than a cell

Oxygen carrier

The protein hemoglobin carries oxygen and gives red blood cells their color. This computer-generated image shows the structure of its molecules. Each molecule contains four iron atoms (yellow). The iron atoms bind oxygen in the lungs, where oxygen is abundant, and release it wherever oxygen is in short supply in the body.

A net of fibrin threads traps the blood cells　*Scab eventually forms over wound*　*Invading germ such as bacteria*　*White blood cell destroys the germs inside the wound*

Epidermis of the skin

Dermis

Platelet

Red blood cell

White blood cell moving to the wound

Blood vessel

Forming blood clots

This cross-section of a skin wound shows how blood reacts. Platelets stick together to form a temporary plug. They also release chemicals that convert a blood protein into threads of fibrin, which trap blood cells to form a jellylike clot. White blood cells destroy invading bacteria. The clot dries out to form a protective scab over the tissues while they repair themselves.

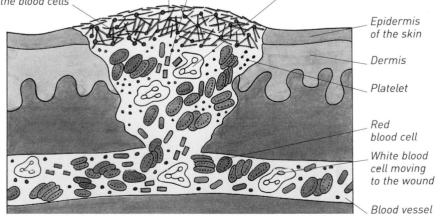

Breathing to live

The body can survive without food or water for some time, but soon dies if breathing stops. Breathing brings fresh air containing oxygen into the lungs, and then expels stale air containing waste carbon dioxide.

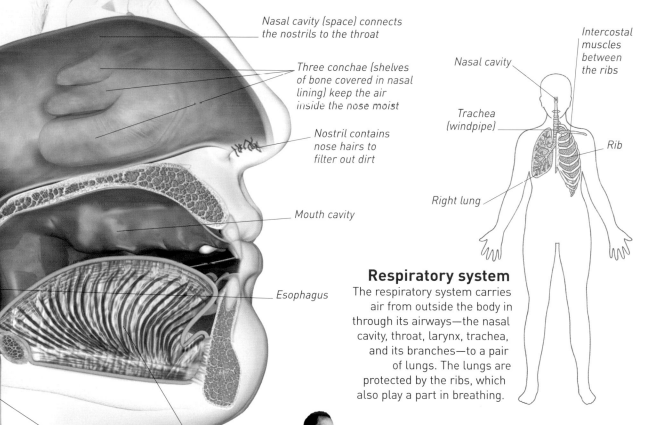

Nasal cavity (space) connects the nostrils to the throat

Three conchae (shelves of bone covered in nasal lining) keep the air inside the nose moist

Nostril contains nose hairs to filter out dirt

Mouth cavity

Esophagus

Tongue

Epiglottis

Vocal cords

Larynx (voice box)

Trachea (windpipe)

Nasal cavity

Intercostal muscles between the ribs

Trachea (windpipe)

Rib

Right lung

Respiratory system

The respiratory system carries air from outside the body in through its airways—the nasal cavity, throat, larynx, trachea, and its branches—to a pair of lungs. The lungs are protected by the ribs, which also play a part in breathing.

Controlled breathing

Musicians like Charlie Parker (left) and Miles Davis need great breath control to play the saxophone, trumpet, and other wind instruments. Precisely timed contractions of the diaphragm and rib muscles push bursts of air out of the mouth and into the instrument. Blowing with varying force and duration produces different notes.

Upper airways

The lungs' delicate tissues are easily damaged by dirt particles, which must be removed in the upper airways after inhalation (breathing in). Nostril hairs filter out larger dirt particles. Sticky mucus covering the nasal lining traps dust and bacteria. The filtered air then passes into the larynx and on to the lungs.

Larynx

During breathing, air passes from the throat, through the larynx, to the trachea (windpipe). The larynx, also called the voice box, is made of nine pieces of cartilage. During swallowing, the entrance to the larynx is covered by a flap of cartilage called the epiglottis, to prevent food from entering the trachea. The vocal cords are two membrane-covered ligaments that produce sound (see below).

Epiglottis covers entrance to the larynx during swallowing

Fat

"Adam's apple" at the front of the thyroid cartilage

Vocal cord

Cartilage ring in trachea

Trachea (windpipe)

Cross-section of the larynx from the side

Inhalation

The lungs cannot move by themselves. For inhalation (breathing in), the diaphragm and intercostal muscles contract to expand the space inside the chest. As the lungs swell to fill the expanded chest, air is sucked in.

Air is sucked in down the trachea

Lung swells

Intercostal muscles pull ribs

Ribs move upward and also outward

Diaphragm contracts and flattens out

Exhalation

For exhalation (breathing out), the diaphragm and intercostal muscles relax. The rib cage falls and the diaphragm is pushed up by the organs below it. This squeezes the lungs, and air is forced back outside.

Lung shrinks

Air is blown out

Ribs move inward and downward

Diaphragm relaxes back into a dome shape

Closed

Open

Vocal cords

Inside the throat, when the vocal cords are relaxed, they open to let air in and out for breathing. To make sounds, they are pulled taut as controlled bursts of air are pushed out, making the closed vocal cords vibrate. The tongue and lips turn sounds into speech.

Breathing and burning

English physician John Mayow (1640–79) showed that if a burning candle and a small animal were put in a sealed jar, the candle went out and the animal died, as part of the air was used up. He realized the same part of air (later named oxygen) was used in the processes of breathing and burning.

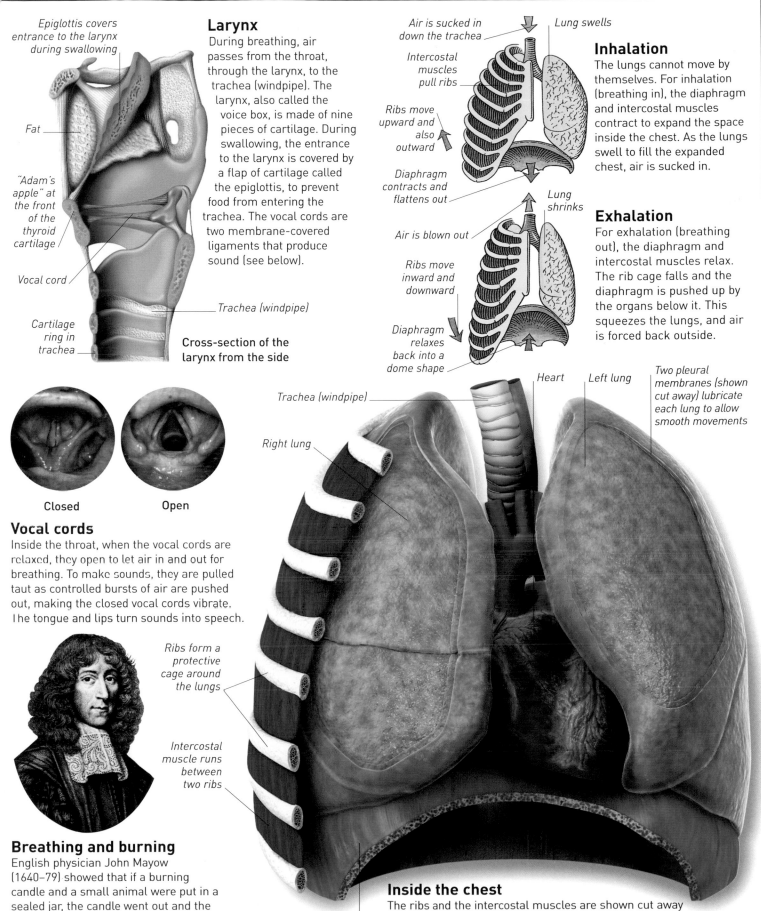

Trachea (windpipe)

Heart

Left lung

Two pleural membranes (shown cut away) lubricate each lung to allow smooth movements

Right lung

Ribs form a protective cage around the lungs

Intercostal muscle runs between two ribs

Diaphragm is a dome-shaped muscle that squeezes the lungs when we breath out

Inside the chest

The ribs and the intercostal muscles are shown cut away to reveal the lungs and diaphragm. When resting, the body breathes at a rate of around 15 times a minute. During exercise, the need for oxygen increases, and so the rate rises up to 50 times a minute.

Inside the lungs

The lungs are filled with millions of microscopic air sacs called alveoli, each wrapped in a mesh of tiny blood vessels. Alveoli take oxygen from the air we breathe in and pass it into the bloodstream, which delivers oxygen to every body cell to release energy from food in a chemical process known as cell respiration. In exchange, the waste product, carbon dioxide, travels in the bloodstream to the alveoli, where it is expelled.

All-over respiration
Italian scientist Lazzaro Spallanzani (1729–99) proposed that respiration took place not just in the lungs, but in every cell of the body. He also discovered that blood delivered oxygen to body tissues and carried away carbon dioxide.

Oxygen gets its name
French chemist Antoine Lavoisier (1743–94) showed that a candle burned using part of the air (a gas he called oxygen) and produced a waste gas (now called carbon dioxide). He suggested animals live by burning food inside the lungs using the oxygen in air—a process he called respiration.

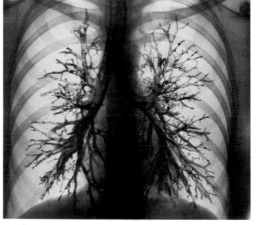

X-ray of the bronchial tree
A branching system of tubes carries air all through the lungs. The trachea divides into two bronchi, one to each lung. Each bronchus splits into many smaller bronchi, then bronchioles, and finally terminal bronchioles, narrower than a hair.

Upper lobe of the right lung

Branch of the right bronchus

Pulmonary artery is colored blue to show it carries oxygen-poor blood

Pulmonary vein is colored red to show it carries oxygen-rich blood

Small bronchus

Terminal (end) bronchioles are the narrowest bronchioles

Middle lobe of the right lung

Bottom lobe of the right lung

Micro-bubbles

This SEM shows red blood cells in a tiny artery in lung tissue. Surrounding the blood vessel are air-filled, bubblelike alveoli, each measuring less than 0.1 mm across.

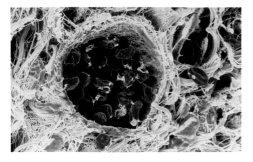

Where gas exchange happens

The lungs' 300 million alveoli provide a combined surface area for gas exchange the size of a tennis-court. Around each alveolus is a network of blood capillaries that exchange gases with the alveolus.

Trachea (windpipe)

Aorta carries oxygen-rich blood from the heart

Pulmonary artery carries oxygen-poor blood to the lungs

Upper lobe of the left lung

Terminal bronchiole

Branch of the pulmonary vein

Branch of the pulmonary artery

Alveoli

Capillary network around the alveolus

Oxygen-poor blood rich in carbon dioxide

Carbon dioxide passes into the alveolus from the blood

Stale air leaves the alveolus by the terminal bronchiole

Gas exchange

The walls of an alveolus and the capillary around it are just 0.001 mm thick. Oxygen from the alveolus passes into the blood. Carbon dioxide moves in the opposite direction.

Oxygen passes from air in the alveolus into the blood

Blood rich in picked-up oxygen

Capillary

Fresh air enters the alveolus from the terminal bronchiole

Lungs and heart

The right lung (here cut away to reveal its airways) has three lobes. The left lung has two and leaves space for the heart. Oxygen-poor blood flows a short distance from the right side of the heart along the pulmonary arteries to the lungs, where it is recharged with oxygen and discharges carbon dioxide. The oxygen-rich blood travels along the pulmonary veins to the heart's left side and is then pumped around the whole body.

Inferior vena cava delivers oxygen-poor blood to the heart

Heart (pp. 42–43)

Descending aorta carries oxygen-rich blood to the lower body

Lower lobe of the left lung

Eating

Eating food is essential for life. Food supplies the nutrients—a mixture of carbohydrates, proteins, fats, and other substances—that give the body energy and provide the building blocks for growth and repair. To release these nutrients, food must be processed both mechanically and chemically, by chewing, swallowing, and digesting.

Parotid salivary gland

Nasal cavity

Soft palate

Parotid duct

Pharynx (throat)

Tongue

Teeth

Sublingual duct

Sublingual salivary gland

Submandibular duct

Submandibular salivary gland

Epiglottis

Esophagus

Trachea (windpipe)

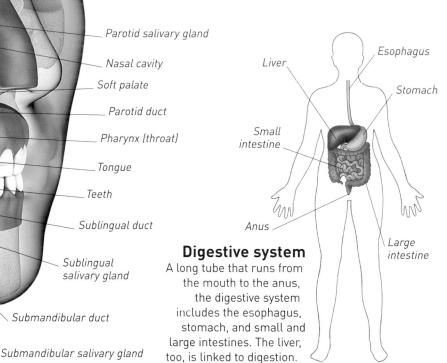

Digestive system

A long tube that runs from the mouth to the anus, the digestive system includes the esophagus, stomach, and small and large intestines. The liver, too, is linked to digestion.

Liver

Esophagus

Stomach

Small intestine

Large intestine

Anus

Inside the mouth

When food enters the mouth, taste buds on the tongue sample it to see how delicious or unpleasant it is. As teeth cut and crush the food, salivary glands squirt watery saliva along ducts into the mouth, to bind and lubricate the food particles together. Saliva also contains an enzyme that starts breaking down starch in the food.

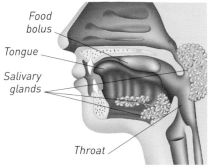

- Food bolus
- Tongue
- Salivary glands
- Throat

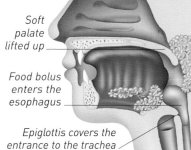

- Soft palate lifted up
- Food bolus enters the esophagus
- Epiglottis covers the entrance to the trachea

- Contracted muscle
- Food bolus
- Relaxed muscle

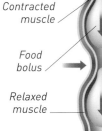

Chewing a mouthful
As we chew, our teeth cut and crush food into small particles. Our tongues mix the food with the sticky mucus in saliva to form a compact, slippery bolus, or ball of food, and push it backward into the throat.

Swallowing
The tongue pushing back triggers the throat muscles to contract, moving the bolus into the esophagus. The soft palate and epiglottis stop food from entering the nasal cavity and trachea.

Peristalsis
Peristalsis, or waves of muscle contractions, squeezes the bolus down the esophagus to the stomach and also through the intestines.

A balanced diet
This meal includes the six main nutrients we need from our food. Rice contains carbohydrates (starches and sugars) for energy. Fish and meat contain proteins that build and maintain the body, plus a little fat, for energy. Vegetables (and fruit) are rich in vitamins and minerals, which help cells work well, and in fiber, which helps the intestinal muscles work better.

Energy release
Running, like any physical activity, requires the energy that comes from food. The digestive process converts food starches into sugars and fats into fatty acids. Broken down inside muscle cells, these fuels release energy for movement.

Teeth

Our teeth break up food to make it easier to swallow and digest. During childhood, baby teeth are replaced by a larger set of adult, or permanent, teeth. These include chisel-like incisors that cut and slice at the front, pointed canines that grip and tear, and flat premolars and molars that crush and grind at the back.

- Enamel is the tooth's hard surface material
- Dentine supports the enamel
- Crown
- Pulp is the soft tissue inside the central cavity
- Gum forms a tight collar around the base of the crown
- Root
- Cement layer secures the root of the tooth in position
- Jawbone
- Blood vessels and nerves supply the living pulp tissue

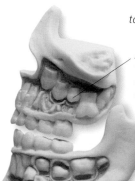

- Root anchors tooth in jawbone
- Adult tooth will push out baby tooth as it grows

- Upper third molar (wisdom tooth) may or may not appear

Five-year teeth
The first 20 baby teeth appear from the age of six months. From about six years they begin to fall out.

Full set of adult teeth
By early adulthood, all 32 adult teeth have come through. Each half jaw has two incisors, one canine, two premolars, and three molars.

Inside a tooth
Bonelike dentine forms the tooth's root and supports a rock-hard crown of nonliving enamel for grinding up food. The central cavity contains living pulp tissue fed by blood vessels and by nerve endings that sense pressure as we bite and chew.

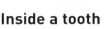

Digestion

After swallowing, it takes about 10 seconds for chewed food to reach the stomach, where digestion really gets under way. The stomach starts to break down food with enzymes (chemical digesters) and churns it into liquid chyme, which it releases slowly into the small intestine. Here, further enzymes digest food into its simplest components. These nutrients are then absorbed into the bloodstream and circulated to the body's cells.

Gastric pits

Millions of gastric pits dot the stomach's lining. Through these tiny holes, gastric glands release gastric juice into the stomach. The juice produces an enzyme that digests the proteins in food. Mucus in the juice coats the stomach lining and prevents the juice from digesting the lining itself.

Food-processor

The stomach is a J-shaped bag that expands as it receives food through the esophagus (gullet) and processes it for the next few hours. Its muscular wall contracts to churn up the food, while acidic gastric (stomach) juice digests the food's proteins. The end result is a soupy liquid called chyme. This is released slowly into the small intestine.

The body's chemical factory

Our largest internal organ, the liver helps balance the chemical makeup of blood. As oxygen-rich blood from the heart and nutrient-rich blood from the intestines pass through the liver, it releases nutrients into the bloodstream for circulation, or stores them for future use. It also makes bile (see below), removes poisons from the blood, destroys bacteria, and recycles worn-out red blood cells. All of this activity generates heat that helps keep the body warm.

The intestines

The small intestine is about 20 ft (6 m) long and has three sections. The short duodenum receives chyme from the stomach and digestive fluids (bile and pancreatic juice) from the liver and pancreas. In the jejunum and ileum, digestion is completed and nutrients are absorbed. The large intestine is just 5 ft (1.5 m) long. Here, watery waste from the ileum dries out as it passes along the colon and forms feces to store in the rectum.

Esophagus

Stomach has a muscular wall

Transverse colon conceals the duodenum connecting the stomach to the jejunum

Jejunum is the middle section of the small intestine

Descending colon

Left lobe of the liver

Right lobe of the liver

Gall bladder stores bile

Ascending colon

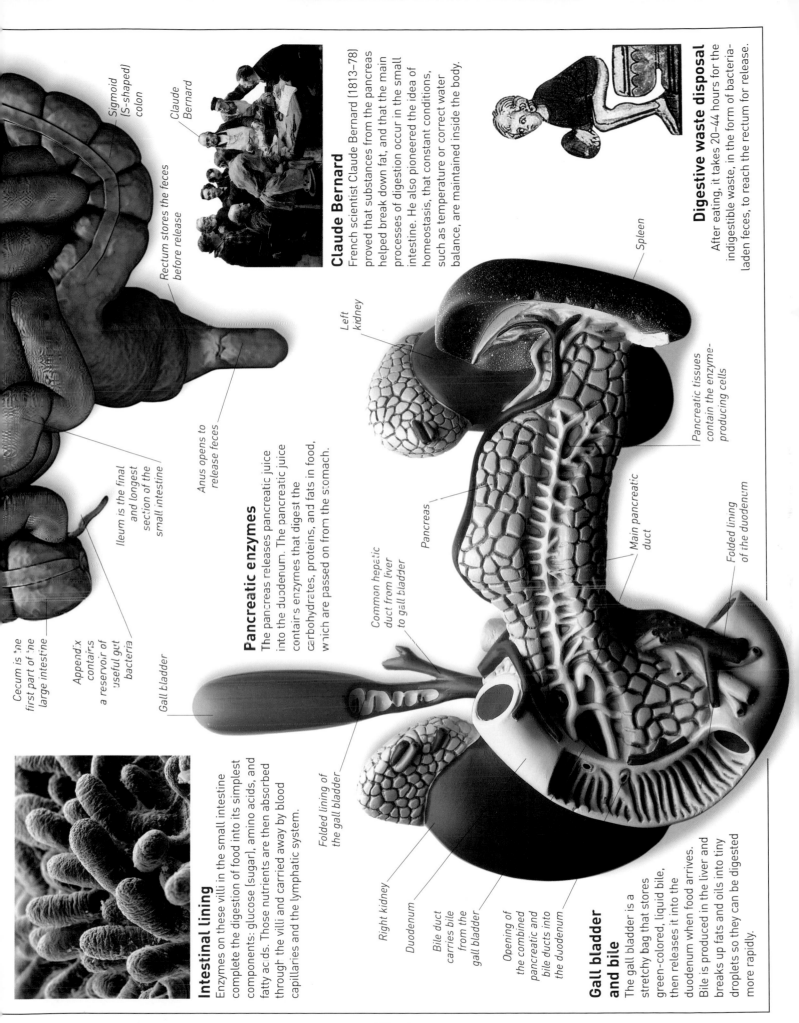

Sigmoid (S-shaped) colon

Claude Bernard

Rectum stores the feces before release

Claude Bernard

French scientist Claude Bernard (1813–78) proved that substances from the pancreas helped break down fat, and that the main processes of digestion occur in the small intestine. He also pioneered the idea of homeostasis, that constant conditions, such as temperature or correct water balance, are maintained inside the body.

Digestive waste disposal

After eating, it takes 20–44 hours for the indigestible waste, in the form of bacteria-laden feces, to reach the rectum for release.

Spleen

Left kidney

Ileum is the final and longest section of the small intestine

Anus opens to release feces

Pancreatic tissues contain the enzyme-producing cells

Pancreas

Main pancreatic duct

Folded lining of the duodenum

Common hepatic duct from liver to gall bladder

Cecum is the first part of the large intestine

Appendix contains a reservoir of useful gut bacteria

Gall bladder

Pancreatic enzymes

The pancreas releases pancreatic juice into the duodenum. The pancreatic juice contains enzymes that digest the carbohydrates, proteins, and fats in food, which are passed on from the stomach.

Folded lining of the gall bladder

Right kidney

Duodenum

Bile duct carries bile from the gall bladder

Opening of the combined pancreatic and bile ducts into the duodenum

Intestinal lining

Enzymes on these villi in the small intestine complete the digestion of food into its simplest components: glucose (sugar), amino acids, and fatty acids. Those nutrients are then absorbed through the villi and carried away by blood capillaries and the lymphatic system.

Gall bladder and bile

The gall bladder is a stretchy bag that stores green-colored, liquid bile, then releases it into the duodenum when food arrives. Bile is produced in the liver and breaks up fats and oils into tiny droplets so they can be digested more rapidly.

Waste disposal

Body cells continually release waste substances, such as urea made by the liver, into the bloodstream. If left to build up, they would poison the body. The urinary system disposes of waste by cleansing the blood as it passes through a pair of kidneys. It also removes excess water to ensure the body's water content stays the same.

Bladder control
When a baby's bladder is full of urine, the stretch receptors in its muscular wall automatically tell it to empty. Young children learn to control this reflex action.

Giant of ancient Greece
The Greek philosopher Aristotle (384–322 BCE) challenged ideas about anatomy by looking inside the real bodies of animals and humans and recording what he saw. He provided the first descriptions of the urinary system and how it works.

Kidney cortex contains blood capillaries and Bowman's capsules

Nephron (filtering unit) consists of a glomerulus and a looping tubule

Capillary reabsorbs nutrients and water from the tubule

Glomerulus inside a Bowman's capsule filters blood

Bowman's capsule

Medulla contains blood vessels and urine-forming tubules

Tubule

U-shaped loop of Henle

Collecting duct

Capsules and loops
English surgeon and scientist William Bowman (1816–92) identified the capsule that bears his name. The U-shaped loop of Henle was later described by the German anatomist Jakob Henle (1809–85).

William Bowman

Small artery entering the glomerulus

Small artery leaving the glomerulus

Filtering unit
Each kidney's blood-filtering unit, or nephron, links to a long tubule. This loops from the cortex to the medulla and back, then joins a collecting duct. As fluid filtered from blood passes along the nephron, useful substances are absorbed back into the bloodstream, leaving waste urine to flow into the collecting duct.

Bowman's capsule
Each capsule surrounds a glomerulus, or cluster of capillaries. They filter the blood and produce a fluid. It contains not only waste, but also substances such as glucose (sugar), which are useful to the body.

Space where filtered fluid collects

Capillary of the glomerulus

Start of tubule

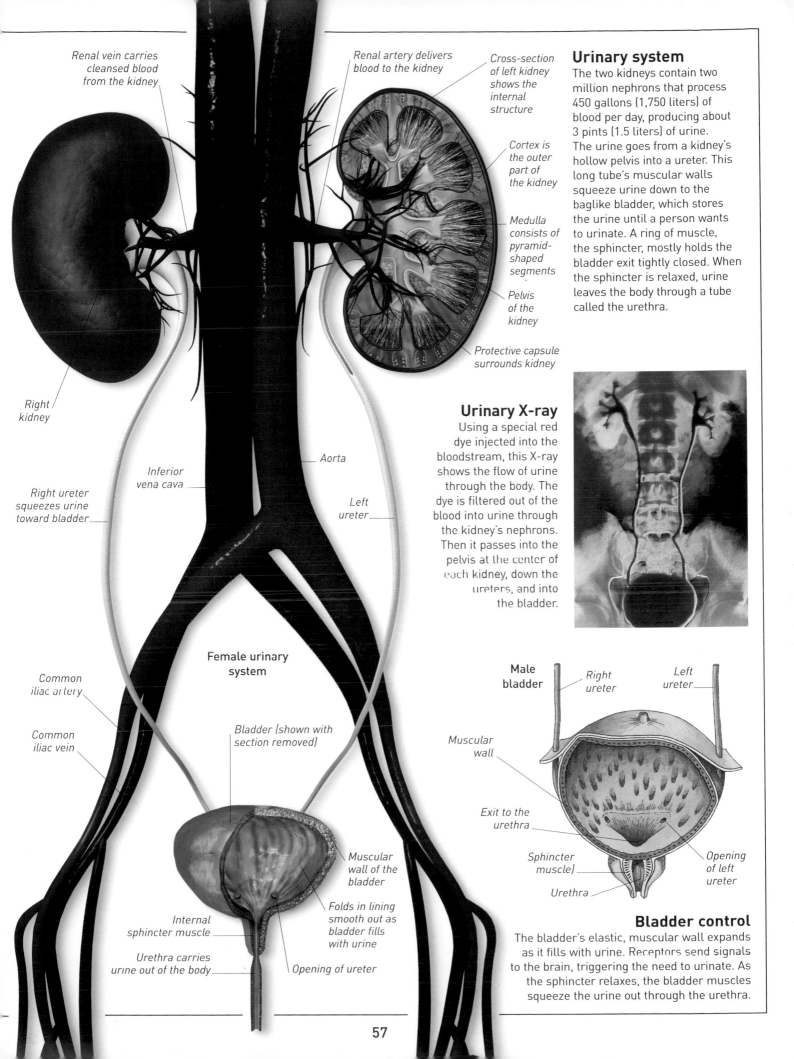

Renal vein carries cleansed blood from the kidney

Renal artery delivers blood to the kidney

Cross-section of left kidney shows the internal structure

Urinary system

The two kidneys contain two million nephrons that process 450 gallons (1,750 liters) of blood per day, producing about 3 pints (1.5 liters) of urine. The urine goes from a kidney's hollow pelvis into a ureter. This long tube's muscular walls squeeze urine down to the baglike bladder, which stores the urine until a person wants to urinate. A ring of muscle, the sphincter, mostly holds the bladder exit tightly closed. When the sphincter is relaxed, urine leaves the body through a tube called the urethra.

Cortex is the outer part of the kidney

Medulla consists of pyramid-shaped segments

Pelvis of the kidney

Right kidney

Protective capsule surrounds kidney

Urinary X-ray

Using a special red dye injected into the bloodstream, this X-ray shows the flow of urine through the body. The dye is filtered out of the blood into urine through the kidney's nephrons. Then it passes into the pelvis at the center of each kidney, down the ureters, and into the bladder.

Right ureter squeezes urine toward bladder

Inferior vena cava

Aorta

Left ureter

Female urinary system

Common iliac artery

Common iliac vein

Bladder (shown with section removed)

Male bladder

Right ureter

Left ureter

Muscular wall

Muscular wall of the bladder

Folds in lining smooth out as bladder fills with urine

Exit to the urethra

Sphincter muscle)

Opening of left ureter

Internal sphincter muscle

Urethra carries urine out of the body

Opening of ureter

Urethra

Bladder control

The bladder's elastic, muscular wall expands as it fills with urine. Receptors send signals to the brain, triggering the need to urinate. As the sphincter relaxes, the bladder muscles squeeze the urine out through the urethra.

Male and female

Like all life-forms, humans reproduce to pass on their genes and continue the cycle of life. Male and female reproductive systems produce different sex cells. Sexual intercourse between a man and a woman brings her eggs and his sperm together. These sex cells contain half of each partner's DNA (genetic instructions), which combine during fertilization inside the woman's body to create a new life. Her uterus then provides the place where the baby will develop.

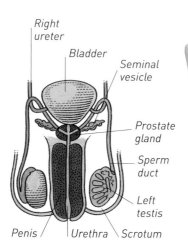

External features

A 1543 guide to anatomy by Vesalius shows the male is more muscular than the female, with wide shoulders, narrow hips, and more facial and body hair. She is more rounded by body fat around the thighs and abdomen, with wide hips and developed breasts.

Right ureter
Bladder
Seminal vesicle
Prostate gland
Sperm duct
Left testis
Penis
Urethra
Scrotum

Front view of the male reproductive system

Male reproductive organs

This side view shows one of two testes that hang outside the body in a skin bag called the scrotum. Inside each testis a hormone stimulates sperm production throughout a man's adult life. During sex, muscle contractions push sperm along two sperm ducts into the urethra and out of the penis.

Bladder
Urethra
Penis
Left testis
Scrotum
Epididymis
Seminal vesicle, together with the prostate gland, adds fluid to the sperm to nourish and stimulate them
Prostate gland

The menstrual cycle

Every 28 days, in a woman's menstrual (monthly) cycle, or period, an egg is released from an ovary and the lining of the uterus thickens to receive the egg if it is fertilized by a sperm. The cycle is controlled by hormones released by the pituitary gland and by ovaries.

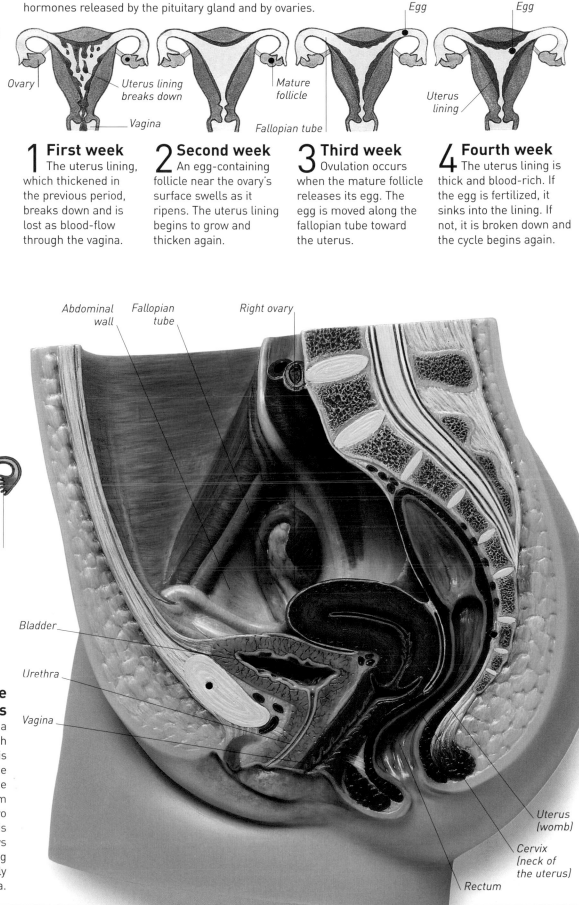

Ovary — Uterus lining breaks down — Vagina — Mature follicle — Fallopian tube — Egg — Egg — Uterus lining

1 First week
The uterus lining, which thickened in the previous period, breaks down and is lost as blood-flow through the vagina.

2 Second week
An egg-containing follicle near the ovary's surface swells as it ripens. The uterus lining begins to grow and thicken again.

3 Third week
Ovulation occurs when the mature follicle releases its egg. The egg is moved along the fallopian tube toward the uterus.

4 Fourth week
The uterus lining is thick and blood-rich. If the egg is fertilized, it sinks into the lining. If not, it is broken down and the cycle begins again.

Regnier de Graaf

Dutch physician and anatomist Regnier de Graaf (1641–73) did detailed research on the male and female reproductive systems. In the female system, he identified the ovaries and described the tiny bubbles on the ovary's surface that appear each month. Later scientists realized that each bubble is a ripe follicle with the much smaller egg contained within it.

Ovary held in position by a ligament — Fallopian tube — Right ovary — Left ovary — Fimbriae — Uterus (womb) — Cervix — Vagina

Front view of the female reproductive system

Female reproductive organs

A woman's ovaries release a single mature egg each month during her fertile years. It is wafted by fimbriae into the fallopian tube that leads to the uterus. If the egg meets a sperm soon after its release, the two fuse and fertilization occurs. This results in a baby that grows inside the greatly expanding uterus (womb) and is eventually born through the vagina.

Abdominal wall — Fallopian tube — Right ovary — Bladder — Urethra — Vagina — Uterus (womb) — Cervix (neck of the uterus) — Rectum

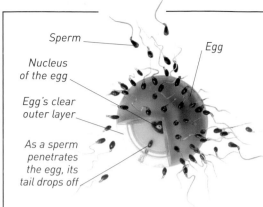

Sperm

Nucleus of the egg

Egg's clear outer layer

Egg

As a sperm penetrates the egg, its tail drops off

Fertilization of an egg

In this cutaway model, one of the sperm trying to get through the outer covering of the egg has succeeded. Its tail has dropped off, and its head (nucleus) will fuse with, or fertilize, the egg's nucleus. No other sperm can now get through.

A new life

Fertilization merges the DNA (genetic instructions) carried by a male sperm and female egg. If the fertilized egg, no bigger than the period at the end of this sentence, settles in the lining of the uterus, it grows into an embryo and then a fetus. Around 38 weeks after fertilization, the fetus is ready to be born. Muscular contractions in the uterus push the baby out through its mother's vagina, and the newborn baby takes its first breath.

Embryo development

The fertilized egg divides into two cells, then four, eight, and so on. A week after fertilization, it implants in the uterus lining, becoming an embryo. As its cells divide, they form muscle, nerve, and other tissues. By five weeks, the embryo is the size of a pea.

Cluster of 16 cells

First embryologist

Italian anatomy professor Hieronymus Fabricius (1537–1619) described the development of unborn babies, or embryos, in humans and in other animals. Known as the founder of embryology, he also named the ovary and predicted its function.

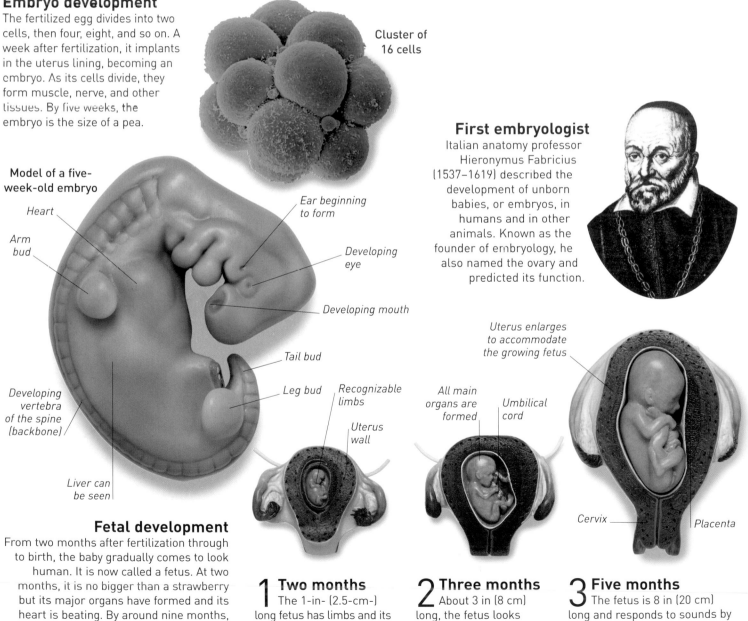

Model of a five-week-old embryo

Heart

Arm bud

Developing vertebra of the spine (backbone)

Liver can be seen

Ear beginning to form

Developing eye

Developing mouth

Tail bud

Leg bud

Recognizable limbs

Uterus wall

All main organs are formed

Umbilical cord

Uterus enlarges to accommodate the growing fetus

Cervix

Placenta

Fetal development

From two months after fertilization through to birth, the baby gradually comes to look human. It is now called a fetus. At two months, it is no bigger than a strawberry but its major organs have formed and its heart is beating. By around nine months, the fetus weighs about 6½–9 lb (3–4 kg).

1 Two months
The 1-in- (2.5-cm-) long fetus has limbs and its brain is expanding rapidly.

2 Three months
About 3 in (8 cm) long, the fetus looks human and has eyes.

3 Five months
The fetus is 8 in (20 cm) long and responds to sounds by kicking and turning somersaults.

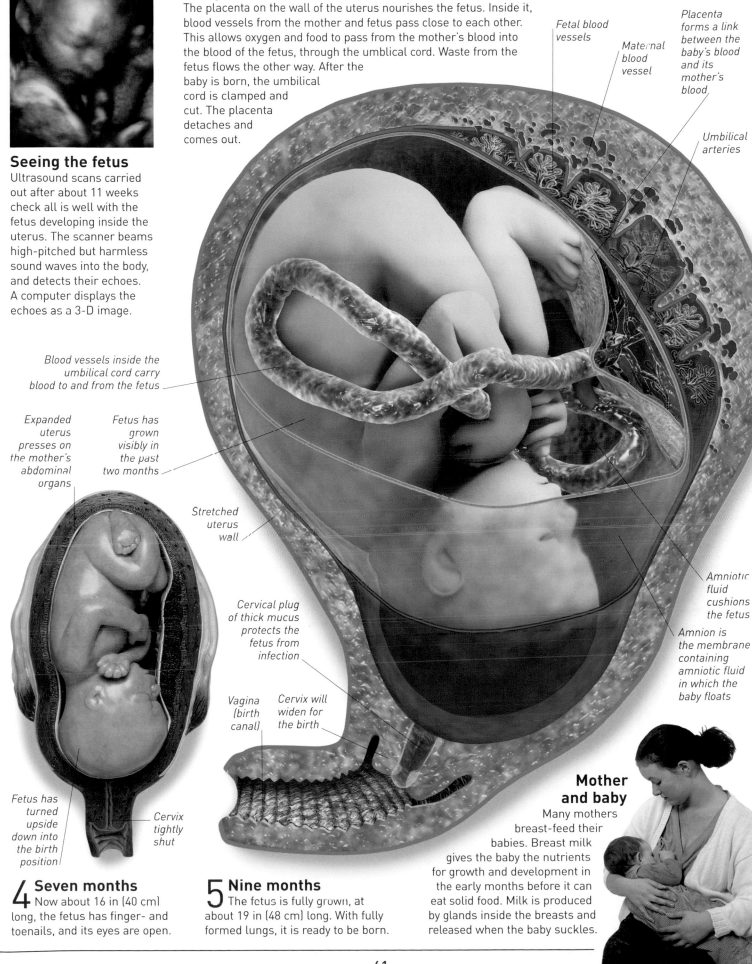

The placenta

The placenta on the wall of the uterus nourishes the fetus. Inside it, blood vessels from the mother and fetus pass close to each other. This allows oxygen and food to pass from the mother's blood into the blood of the fetus, through the umbilical cord. Waste from the fetus flows the other way. After the baby is born, the umbilical cord is clamped and cut. The placenta detaches and comes out.

Fetal blood vessels

Maternal blood vessel

Placenta forms a link between the baby's blood and its mother's blood

Umbilical arteries

Seeing the fetus

Ultrasound scans carried out after about 11 weeks check all is well with the fetus developing inside the uterus. The scanner beams high-pitched but harmless sound waves into the body, and detects their echoes. A computer displays the echoes as a 3-D image.

Blood vessels inside the umbilical cord carry blood to and from the fetus

Expanded uterus presses on the mother's abdominal organs

Fetus has grown visibly in the past two months

Stretched uterus wall

Amniotic fluid cushions the fetus

Amnion is the membrane containing amniotic fluid in which the baby floats

Cervical plug of thick mucus protects the fetus from infection

Vagina (birth canal)

Cervix will widen for the birth

Fetus has turned upside down into the birth position

Cervix tightly shut

4 Seven months

Now about 16 in (40 cm) long, the fetus has finger- and toenails, and its eyes are open.

5 Nine months

The fetus is fully grown, at about 19 in (48 cm) long. With fully formed lungs, it is ready to be born.

Mother and baby

Many mothers breast-feed their babies. Breast milk gives the baby the nutrients for growth and development in the early months before it can eat solid food. Milk is produced by glands inside the breasts and released when the baby suckles.

Growth and development

From birth to old age, we follow the same pattern of growth and body development. Physical and mental changes turn us from children into adults, and growth stops by our early 20s. The body then matures, and in later years begins to deteriorate. This pattern is controlled, like all of the body's processes, by 23 pairs of chromosomes in the nucleus of every body cell. Each chromosome is made up of deoxyribonucleic acid (DNA). Sections of DNA, called genes, contain the coded instructions that build and maintain the body.

Master molecule
US biologist James Watson (1928–) and British biophysicist Francis Crick (1916–2004) showed that the DNA molecule has two strands that spiral like a twisted ladder. Its rungs hold the code forming the instructions in genes.

Genes and inheritance
If a man and woman reproduce, they each pass on a set of genes to their child. The genes that this girl inherited from her mother and father are mostly identical, but some are different, so her combination of genes is unique.

Cell division
Bodies grow by making new cells. Cells reproduce by dividing in two. For most cells, this involves mitosis. Each chromosome duplicates inside a parent cell to produce an identical copy. The copies move apart, and the cell divides to produce two daughter cells that are identical to each other.

Daughter cell grows after division

Nucleus of daughter cell contains 46 chromosomes

Cell's cytoplasm splits to separate daughter cells

Human genome
Every human cell contains 23 chromosomes, called the genome. Each has a partner. One of each pair is from the mother, one is from the father. Each chromosome has the same genes as its partner, but not always identical versions. It might carry the version of a gene giving blue eyes, but the other chromosome might have the version for brown. While 22 of the chromosome pairs match, the 23rd pair matches only in females and determines a person's sex.

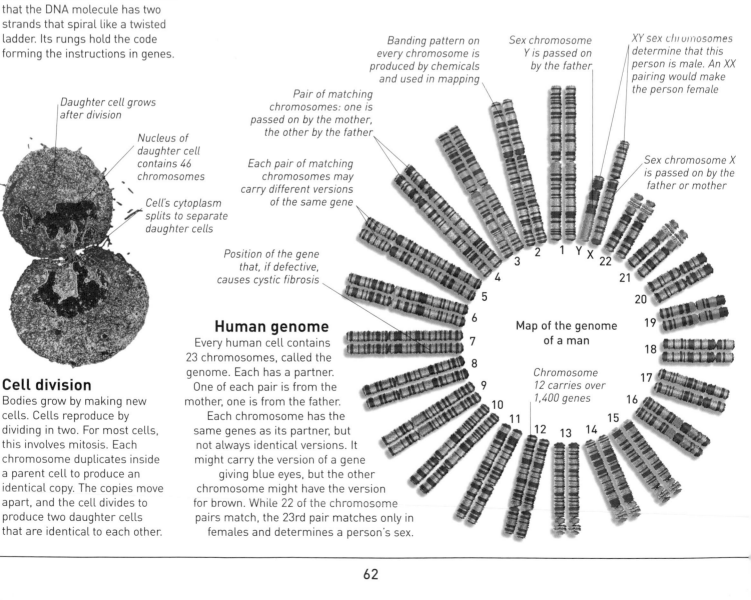

Banding pattern on every chromosome is produced by chemicals and used in mapping

Sex chromosome Y is passed on by the father

XY sex chromosomes determine that this person is male. An XX pairing would make the person female

Pair of matching chromosomes: one is passed on by the mother, the other by the father

Each pair of matching chromosomes may carry different versions of the same gene

Sex chromosome X is passed on by the father or mother

Position of the gene that, if defective, causes cystic fibrosis

Map of the genome of a man

Chromosome 12 carries over 1,400 genes

2 1 Y X 22
3
4 21
5 20
6 19
7 18
8 17
9 16
10 15
11 14
12 13

Growth and the skeleton

Before birth, the skeleton is made up of either flexible cartilage or, in the skull, membranes reinforced with fibers. As the fetus grows, most of these tissues are ossified—replaced by hard bone. But the bones of the cranium (skull) are incomplete at birth and are connected by fontanelles, or membranes, that allow the brain to grow. By early childhood, these too are ossified, and the skull bones are knitted together. During childhood, the skull's facial bones grow rapidly to catch up with the cranium.

Anterior fontanelle

Mastoid fontanelle

Fetal skull

Small facial bones

Sphenoidal fontanelle

Puberty and adolescence

During the three to four years of puberty, the body grows rapidly and the reproductive system begins to function. Most girls reach puberty at 10–12 years, and boys at 12–14 years. A girl's body becomes more rounded, she develops breasts, and her periods start. A boy's body becomes more muscular, his voice deepens, facial hair grows, and he starts producing sperm. Puberty forms part of adolescence, the process that also involves mental changes as teenagers turn into adults.

Cranial bones have ossified completely

Facial bones grow rapidly during childhood

Adult tooth pushing out the baby tooth

Lower jaw greatly increased in size

Six-year-old skull

Jigsawlike, fixed suture joint

Later years

In our fifties, aging becomes noticeable. The skin loses its springiness and develops lines and wrinkles, as in the face of this elderly American Indian. The heart and lungs become less efficient, joints stiffen and bones become more fragile, vision is less effective, and brain function decreases. But looking after the body with healthy food and exercise can slow these changes and help us stay healthy into our eighties.

Chief of the Crow tribe (c. 1906)

Suture joints still visible in adult skull

Adult skull

Young adulthood

Middle age

Old age

Puberty and adolescence

Birth

Death

Facial bones have grown larger still

Tooth missing, possibly from decay

Life story from cradle to grave

Following birth and childhood, early adulthood is a time of responsibility and becoming a parent. Middle age brings wisdom, and the start of aging. In old age, the body begins to decline until, eventually, we die. With better food, health care, and sanitation in the developed world, average life expectancy is almost 80 years, twice that of the 16th-century man above.

Future bodies

Advances in biology, medicine, and technology make it possible to repair or improve the human body in new ways, such as bionic limbs and artificial organs. For some people, research using stem cells or hybrid embryos interferes with the sanctity of life. Others predict a world of nanobots, cyborgs, and brain microchips.

Stem cells taken from umbilical cord blood

Stem cells
Doctors believe unspecialized cells, called stem cells, can be used to repair diseased or damaged tissues in patients. Stem cells divide to produce a range of cell types and so can build many types of body tissue.

Gene therapy
Each body cell contains over 20,000 genes, the DNA instructions that build and run it. A faulty gene can cause disease. Scientists hope it will soon be possible to cure some conditions using gene therapy—replacing faulty genes with normal ones carried into body cells by a harmless virus.

Designer children
One day it may be possible to treat a sick child with a faulty gene by using stem cells from a specially designed sibling. First, a number of embryos are created through IVF (in vitro fertilization), where an egg is fertilized outside the body in a laboratory. If it does not have the faulty gene, it is placed in the mother's uterus to develop into a baby. When the designer child is born, stem cells in its discarded umbilical cord are used to treat its sick sibling.

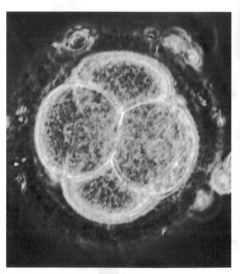

Hybrid embryos
Human embryos are a controversial source of stem cells. As an alternative, the DNA-containing nucleus in a cow's egg is replaced by a nucleus from a human skin cell. The cell divides to create a hybrid embryo that is 99.9 percent human and is a new source of stem cells to research cures for diseases.

Bionic arm is wired
to the chest muscles

Sensors monitor
signals from the
chest muscles and
trigger arm and
hand movements

Artificial hand
and fingers
move according
to the woman's
conscious
thoughts

Growing organs

Currently, diseased organs are replaced by
transplanting a donor organ from someone
else. Using cells from the patient instead,
bladder tissue has been grown around a
mold (above) and the new bladder was
successfully implanted into the patient.

Bionic limbs

After this patient lost her arm in an accident,
a bionic arm was wired to her chest muscles.
When she thinks about moving her hand,
messages travel to the muscles, which send out
electrical signals. Sensors pass these to a tiny
computer that tells her arm how to move.

Neuron is one
of a network
forming a
circuit with
a microchip

Pillar supports
the neuron on
the microchip

Brain microchips

This microchip forms a
miniature electronic circuit
with a network of neurons
and can stimulate them to
send and receive signals to one
another and to the microchip.
Future scientists might use
neuron–microchip circuits to
repair brain damage or boost
memory or intelligence.

Medical nanobots

Nanotechnology manipulates atoms
and molecules to build tiny machines.
These nanobots, or nanorobots, are
self-propelled, respond to their
surroundings, and can carry out tasks
on their own initiative. One day, it may
be possible for medical nanobots to
detect, diagnose, and repair damage
to the body's cells and tissues.

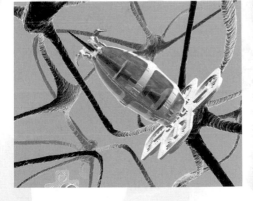

Cyborgs

In the *Terminator* films, actor
Arnold Schwarzenegger played
the role of a cyborg—a character
with increased natural abilities,
being part-human, part-machine.
Future advances in technology may
yet make such hybrids possible.

Eternal life?

Medical advances, such as
gene therapy and organ
replacement, together
with lifestyle changes,
could enable everyone
to live longer. But what
quality of life would there
be for a 150-year-old?
And how would our
crowded planet support
so many extra, possibly
unproductive, human beings?

Timeline

With each new discovery, scientists have built up a clearer picture of the body and its systems. Even so, there remain many mysteries about the workings of the human body.

c. 160,000 BCE
Modern humans first appear.

c. 2650 BCE
Egyptian Imhotep is the earliest known physician.

c. 1500 BCE
The earliest known medical text, the *Ebers Papyrus*, is written in Egypt.

c. 500 BCE
Greek physician Alcmaeon suggests that brain, and not heart, is the seat of thought and feelings.

c. 420 BCE
Greek physician Hippocrates emphasizes the importance of diagnosis.

c. 280 BCE
Herophilus of Alexandria describes the cerebrum and cerebellum of brain.

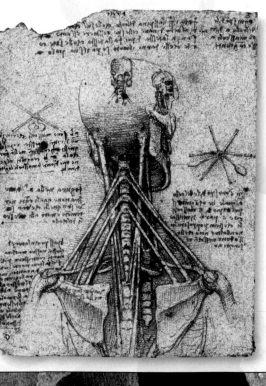

Statue of Imhotep c. 2650 BCE

c. 200 CE
Greek-born Roman doctor Claudius Galen describes, incorrectly, how the human body works; his teachings are not challenged until the 1500s.

c. 1025
Persian doctor Avicenna publishes the *Canon of Medicine*, which will influence European medicine for the next 500 years.

c. 1280
Syrian doctor Ibn an-Nafis shows that blood circulates around the body.

c. 1316
Italian anatomist Mondino dei Liuzzi publishes his dissection guide *Anatomy*.

c. 1500
Italian artist and scientist Leonardo da Vinci makes anatomical drawings based on his own dissections.

Anatomical drawing by Leonardo da Vinci

1543
Flemish doctor Andreas Vesalius publishes *On the Structure of the Human Body*, which accurately describes human anatomy.

1562
Italian anatomist Bartolomeo Eustachio describes the ear in *The Examination of the Organ of Hearing*

1590
Dutch eyeglass-maker, Zacharias Janssen, invents the microscope.

1603
Hieronymus Fabricius, an Italian anatomist, describes the structure of a vein in his book, *On the Valves of Veins*.

1628
English doctor William Harvey describes blood circulation in *On the Movement of the Heart and Blood in Animals*.

1662
French philosopher René Descartes' book, *Treatise of Man*, describes the human body as a machine.

1663
Italian biologist Marcello Malpighi discovers capillaries, the small blood vessels that link arteries and veins.

1664
English doctor Thomas Willis describes the blood supply to the brain.

1665
English physicist Robert Hooke coins the term "cell" for the smallest units of life he sees through his compound microscope.

1672
Dutch anatomist Regnier de Graaf describes the female reproductive system.

Hooke's microscope, 1665

1674–77
Antoni van Leeuwenhoek, a Dutch cloth merchant and microscope-maker, describes human blood cells and sperm cells.

1691
English doctor Clopton Havers describes the microscopic structure of bones.

1775
French chemist Antoine Lavoisier discovers oxygen and later shows that cell respiration consumes oxygen.

1800
French doctor Marie-François Bichat shows that organs are made of groups of cells called tissues.

1811
Scottish anatomist Charles Bell shows that nerves are bundles of nerve cells.

1816
French doctor René Laënnec invents the stethoscope to listen to the lungs and heart.

1833
American army surgeon William Beaumont publishes the results of his experiments into the mechanism of digestion.

1837
Czech biologist Johannes Purkinje observes neurons in the brain's cerebellum.

1842
British surgeon William Bowman describes the microscopic structure and workings of the kidney.

1848
French scientist Claude Bernard describes the workings of the liver.

An early ophthalmoscope

1851
German physicist Hermann von Helmholtz invents the ophthalmoscope, an instrument for looking inside the eye.

1861
French doctor Paul Pierre Broca identifies the area on the brain that controls speech.

1871
German scientist Wilhelm Kühne coins the term "enzyme" for substances that speed up chemical reactions inside living things.

1895
German physicist Wilhelm Roentgen discovers X-rays.

1901
Karl Landsteiner, an Austrian-American doctor, identifies blood groups, paving the way for more successful blood transfusions.

1905
British scientist Ernest Starling coins the term "hormone."

1930
American physiologist Walter Cannon coins the term "homeostasis" for mechanisms that maintain a stable state inside the body.

1933
German electrical engineer Ernst Ruska invents the electron microscope.

1952
US surgeon Joseph E. Murray performs the first kidney transplant, on identical twins.

1952
In the US, Paul Zoll invents the pacemaker to control an irregular heartbeat.

A wounded US soldier receives a blood transfusion during World War II

1953
US biologist James Watson and British physicist Francis Crick discover the double-helix structure of DNA.

1958
British doctor Ian Donald uses ultrasound scanning to check the health of a fetus.

1961
US scientist Marshall Nirenberg cracks the genetic code of DNA.

1967
Magnetic resonance imaging (MRI) is first used to see soft tissues inside the body.

1972
Computed tomography (CT) scanning first produces images of human organs.

1980
Doctors perform "keyhole" surgery inside the body through small incisions with the assistance of an endoscope.

1980s
Positron emission tomography (PET) scans first produce images of brain activity.

1982
The first artificial heart, invented by US scientist Robert Jarvik, is transplanted into a patient.

1984
French scientist Luc Montagnier discovers the human immunodeficiency virus (HIV) that results in AIDS.

Blood bag

2001
Scientists perform the first germline gene transfer in animals, to prevent faulty genes from being passed to offspring.

2002
Gene therapy is used to treat an inherited immunodeficiency disease that leaves the body unable to fight infection.

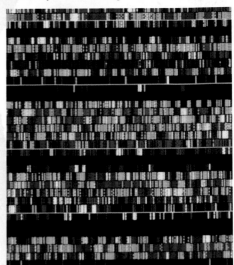

Computer display of DNA sequencing

2003
Scientists publish results of the Human Genome Project, identifying the DNA sequence of a full set of chromosomes.

2006
A urinary bladder, grown in the laboratory from a patient's own cells, is successfully transplanted to replace a damaged organ.

2007
Previously thought to be useless, the appendix is shown to hold a backup reservoir of bacteria that is essential to the workings of the large intestine.

2008
Dutch geneticist Marjolein Kreik becomes the first woman to have her genome sequenced.

2010
DaVinci, a surgical robot, performs the world's first all-robotic surgery in Montreal, Canada.

Surgical robot, DaVinci

2013
Scientists in Japan create a functional human liver from skin and blood stem cells.

Find out more

Look for news stories about the latest discoveries in medical science, and documentaries about the human body and how it works. Check for special exhibitions at museums near you, or search in your local library and online. You also have your own body to study! Take good care of it by eating a balanced diet and exercising regularly.

The old operating room
This 19th-century operating room at the old site of St. Thomas' hospital in London predates anesthetics. Surgeons worked quickly to minimize a patient's suffering during amputations and other operations. Medical students watched from tiered stands around the operating table.

Anatomy on show

Body Worlds is a touring display of "plastinates"—real human bodies that are cleverly preserved in exciting poses to reveal inner organs and tissues. Since 1995, more than 20 million people have seen the exhibition worldwide.

Skin is removed to reveal the muscles, major organs, and blood vessels

One of the plastinates at the *Body Worlds* exhibition

Walk-in body

At the Health Museum in Houston, Texas, visitors can take a larger-than-life tour through the human body—including this arch created by a giant backbone and ribs. The Amazing Body Pavilion features exciting interactive experiences including a giant eyeball and a walk-through brain, and hands-on exhibits about health and well-being.

Giant body sculpture

Australian artist Ron Mueck's *Mask II* is a giant self-portrait of the artist sleeping and is sculpted from resin and fiberglass. Visits to art galleries to see sculptures and paintings can reveal much about the variety of the human form.

Acrobat's brain controls balance, posture, and precise movements

ACROBATICS

Watching ballet and circus shows like the *Cirque du Soleil* provides a great opportunity to marvel at the strength, flexibility, and grace of the human body.

Muscle and joint flexibility is achieved by constant training

PLACES TO VISIT

FRANKLIN INSTITUTE
PHILADELPHIA, PENNSYLVANIA

The Giant Heart is a 5,000 square-foot walk-through exhibit; the heart pulses with interactive devices areas. The museum also includes The Melting Humans exhibit, which shows internal organs and systems.

HALL OF SCIENCE
NEW YORK, NEW YORK

Lots of hands-on exhibits allow visitors to explore perceptions, molecules, and health. A highlight is an infrared camera that maps your body's hot spots.

THE SCIENCE MUSEUM OF MINNESOTA
ST. PAUL, MINNESOTA

The human body gallery explores how our bodies work. Blood flow, cellular biology, disease, and DNA are explained with super-sized models and hands-on activities.

CARNEGIE SCIENCE CENTER
PITTSBURGH, PENNSYLVANIA

Did you ever want to be a surgeon? The Body Tech exhibit gives you a chance to learn about some of the latest sugical techniques and to try your hand at some of the skills that surgeons use.

Early stethoscope at the Science Museum, London

USEFUL WEBSITES

- A fun, animated guide to the human body:
  www.brainpop.com/health
- The site's hundreds of interactive anatomy pictures let you explore the human body like never before:
  www.innerbody.com
- A website for children, with tips on keeping the body healthy:
  kidshealth.org/kids
- This website from the BBC covers all aspects of the body:
  www.bbc.co.uk/science/humanbody

Glossary

Blood vessels supplying the lower arm and hand

ABDOMEN The lower part of the torso between the chest and hips.

ADOLESCENCE The period of physical and mental changes that occurs during the teenage years and marks the transition from childhood to adulthood.

ALVEOLI The microscopic air bags in the lungs through which oxygen enters the blood and carbon dioxide leaves it.

AMNIOTIC FLUID A liquid that surrounds the fetus inside its mother's uterus. It protects the fetus from knocks and jolts.

ANATOMY The study of the structure of the human body.

ANTIBODY A substance released by cells called lymphocytes that marks an invading pathogen or germ for destruction.

ARTERY A blood vessel that carries blood from the heart toward the body tissues.

ATOM The smallest particle of an element, such as carbon or hydrogen, that can exist.

BACTERIA A type of microorganism. Some bacteria are pathogens (germs) that cause disease in humans.

BILE A fluid delivered from the liver to the intestine to aid digestion.

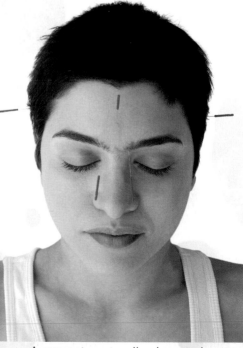

Acupuncture needles inserted into the skin to provide pain relief

BLOOD VESSEL A tube, such as an artery, vein, or capillary, that transports blood around the body.

CAPILLARY A microscopic blood vessel that links arteries to veins.

CARTILAGE A tough, flexible tissue that supports the nose, ears, and other body parts and covers bones' ends in joints.

CELL One of the trillions of microscopic living units that make up a human body.

CHROMOSOME One of 46 packages of DNA found inside most body cells.

CHYME A souplike liquid that is formed of part-digested food in the stomach and released into the small intestine.

DIAPHRAGM The dome-shaped muscle between the thorax and the abdomen.

DIGESTION The breakdown of the complex molecules in food into simple nutrients, such as sugars, which are absorbed into the bloodstream and used by cells.

DISSECTION The careful cutting open of a dead body to study its internal structure.

DNA (DEOXYRIBONUCLEIC ACID) A molecule containing genes (instructions) for building and running the body's cells.

EMBRYO An unborn baby during the first eight weeks of development after fertilization.

ENDOCRINE GLAND A collection of cells, such as the thyroid gland, that release hormones into the bloodstream.

ENZYME A protein that acts as a biological catalyst to speed up the rate of chemical reactions inside and outside cells.

Model of an enzyme involved in digesting food

FECES The semisolid waste made up of undigested food, dead cells, and bacteria, removed from the body through the anus.

FERTILIZATION The fusion of a sperm and an egg to make a new human being.

FETUS A baby growing inside the uterus from its ninth week until its birth.

FOLLICLE A group of cells inside an ovary that surrounds and nurtures an egg. Also a pit in the skin from which a hair grows.

GAS EXCHANGE The movement of oxygen from the lungs into the bloodstream, and of carbon dioxide from the bloodstream into the lungs.

GENE One of 20,000–25,000 instructions contained within a cell's chromosomes that control its construction and operation.

GLAND A group of cells that creates chemical substances, such as hormones or sweat, and releases them into the body.

GLUCOSE A type of sugar that circulates in the blood and provides cells with their major source of energy.

HOMEOSTASIS The maintenance of stable conditions, such as temperature or amount of water or glucose, inside the body so that cells can work normally.

HORMONE A chemical messenger that is made by an endocrine gland and carried in the blood to its target tissue or organ.

IMMUNE SYSTEM A collection of cells in the circulatory and lymphatic systems that track and destroy pathogens (germs).

KERATIN The tough, waterproof protein in cells that make up the hair, nails, and upper epidermis of the skin.

LYMPH The fluid that flows through the lymphatic system from tissues to the blood.

MEMBRANE A thin layer of tissue that covers or lines an external or internal body surface. Also a cell's outer layer.

MENINGES The protective membranes that cover the brain and spinal cord.

MENSTRUAL CYCLE The sequence of bodily changes, repeated roughly every 28 days, that prepares a woman's reproductive system to receive a fertilized egg.

METABOLISM The chemical processes that take place in every cell in the body, resulting, for example, in the release of energy and growth.

MOLECULE A tiny particle that is made up of two or more linked atoms.

NEURON One of the billions of nerve cells that make up the nervous system.

Neurons carry electrical signals in the body's communication network

SURGERY The treatment of disease or injury by direct intervention, often using surgical instruments to open the body.

SUTURE An immovable joint such as that between two skull bones.

SYNAPSE A junction between two neurons, where a nerve signal is passed from cell to cell. The neurons are very close at a synapse, but they do not touch.

SYSTEM A collection of linked organs that work together to perform a specific task or tasks. An example is the digestive system.

TISSUE An organized group of one type of cell, or similar types of cells, that works together to perform a particular function.

TORSO The central part of the body, also known as the trunk, made up of the thorax and abdomen.

UMBILICAL CORD The ropelike structure that connects a fetus to the placenta.

URINE A liquid produced by the kidneys that contains wastes, surplus water, and salts removed from the blood.

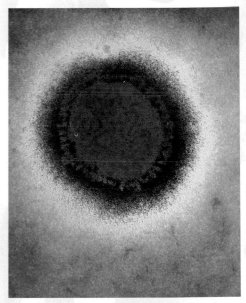

TEM of an influenza (flu) virus magnified 135,000 times

NUTRIENT A substance, such as glucose (sugar), needed in the diet to maintain normal body functioning and good health.

OLFACTORY To do with the sense of smell.

ORGAN A body part, such as the heart, that is made up of two or more types of tissue and performs a particular function.

OSSIFICATION The formation of bone, replacing cartilage with bone tissue.

PATHOGEN A germ, a type of microorganism, such as a bacterium or virus, that causes disease in humans.

PHYSICIAN A doctor.

PHYSIOLOGY The study of the body's functions and processes—how it works.

PLACENTA The organ that delivers food and oxygen to a fetus from its mother. Half develops from the mother's body, and half is part of the fetus's body.

PREGNANCY The period of time between an embryo implanting in the uterus and a baby being born, usually 38–40 weeks.

Sutures, or jigsawlike joints in the skull

PUBERTY The part of adolescence when a child's body changes into an adult's and the reproductive system starts to work.

SPERM Male sex cells, also called spermatozoa.

SPINAL CORD A column of nervous tissue inside the spine. It relays nerve signals between the brain and body.

VEIN A blood vessel that carries blood from the body tissues toward the heart.

VIRUS A nonliving pathogen that causes diseases, such as colds and measles, in humans.

X-RAY A form of radiation that reveals bones when projected through the body onto film.

Index

A

acupuncture 9, 70
adolescence 63, 70
adrenal glands 40
aging 63
alveoli 50, 51, 70
amniotic fluid 61, 70
anatomy 6, 10–11, 70
antibodies 45, 70
Aristotle 56
arms 16, 17, 24, 65
arteries 10, 42, 43, 44, 45, 70
atoms 13, 70
Avicenna 8, 9, 66

B

babies 59, 60–61, 62, 64
backbone 16
bacteria 12, 45, 55, 70
Baglivi, Giorgio 22
balance 25, 37
Banting, Sir Frederick 41
Beethoven, Ludwig van 36
Bernard, Claude 55, 67
Best, Charles 41
bile 54, 55, 70
bionic limbs 65
birth 60, 61
bladder 56, 57, 58, 59, 65
blood 9, 46–47, 66
blood clots 47
blood groups 47
blood transfusions 46, 47
blood vessels 6, 19, 29, 33, 44–45, 70
bone marrow 18, 19
bones 6, 16–21, 24, 37
Bowman, William 56, 67
Braille 32
brain 25, 26, 28–31, 65, 66, 67
brain stem 26, 27, 28, 30, 31
breathing 48–51
Broca, Paul Pierre 29, 67

C

capillaries 44, 45, 66, 70
carbon dioxide 48, 50
cartilage 16, 18, 20, 21, 70
cells 7, 12–13, 19, 62, 64, 70
central nervous system 26
cerebellum 26, 27, 28, 30
cerebral cortex 29, 31
cerebrum 26, 27, 28–31
Cesalpino, Andrea 42
Charcot, Jean-Martin 27
Chauliac, Guy de 16
chromosomes 7, 62, 70
chyme 54, 70
circulatory system 44–45
collagen 19, 21
computed tomography (CT) 14, 67
coronary circulation 42
Crick, Francis 62, 67
cyborgs 65

D

diabetes 41
diaphragm 27, 49, 70
digestion 7, 52–55, 70
diseases 8, 45, 64
dissection 6, 10–11, 66, 70
DNA 7, 58, 60, 62, 64, 67, 70
dreams 31

E

ears 36–37
eating 52–53
eggs 58, 59, 60
electron microscopes 13
embalming 8
embryo 18, 60, 64, 70
emotions 31
endocrine system 40–41, 70
endoscopy 15
enzymes 41, 52, 54, 55, 70
epiglottis 48, 49, 53
Eustachio, Bartolomeo 36, 66
eyes 34–35

F

Fabricius, Hieronymus 60, 66
facial muscles 25
feces 54, 55, 70
feet 16, 21
fertilization 59, 60, 70
fetus 15, 60–61, 63, 70
fingerprints 32, 33
follicles 32, 33, 70
food 52–55
Freud, Sigmund 30

G

Galen, Claudius 8, 9, 10, 66
gall bladder 54, 55
gas exchange 51, 70
genes 7, 62, 64, 70
glands 40–41, 70
glial cells 30
glucose 40, 41, 54, 56, 70
Graaf, Regnier de 59, 66
growth 62–63

H

hair 32, 33
Haller, Albrecht von 44
hands 17, 20, 24, 32, 33
Harvey, William 44, 66
hearing 36–37
heart 6, 42–43, 44, 49, 51
Helmholtz, Hermann von 35, 67
hemoglobin 47
Henle, Jakob 56
hip joint 18, 20
Hippocrates 8, 9, 66
homeostasis 55, 70
Hooke, Robert 12, 66
hormones 40–41, 70
hybrid embryos 64
hypothalamus 30, 40, 41

I J

immune system 45, 46, 70
infections 45
Ingrassias, Giovanni 19
inheritance 62
insulin 41
intelligence 6, 30
intestines 7, 54–55
joints 20–21

K L

keratin 32, 33, 70
kidneys 40, 56–57
knee 20, 21
Landsteiner, Karl 47, 67
larynx 21, 48, 49
Lavoisier, Antoine 50, 66
Leeuwenhoek, Antoni van 12, 66
lifespan 63, 65
ligaments 20, 21, 24
limbic system 30, 31
Liuzzi, Mondino dei 10, 66
liver 52, 54, 56, 67
lungs 6, 42, 43, 48–51
lymph 45, 70
lymphatic system 44, 45
lymphocytes 41, 45, 46, 47

M

macrophages 45
magnetic resonance imaging (MRI) 15, 67
Malpighi, Marcello 12, 66
medicine 8, 9, 64–65
melanin 33, 35
membranes 13, 63, 70
menstrual cycle 59, 70
metabolism 13, 40, 70
microscopes 12–13, 66, 67
milk 52
molecules 7, 70
mouth 52–53
mummies 8–9, 42
muscles 6, 22–25

N

nails 9, 32, 33
nanobots 65
nerves 6, 22, 25, 26–27, 35, 37, 38, 39
nervous system 26–27, 28
neurons 22, 26, 27, 28, 30, 38, 65, 70, 71
nose 38, 48
nutrients 52, 53, 54, 55, 61, 71

O

ophthalmoscopes 14, 35
organs 7, 40, 71
ossification 63, 71
ovaries 40, 58, 59
oxygen 6, 42, 43, 46, 47, 48–49, 50–51

P Q

pancreas 40, 41, 55
pathogens 45, 71
Pavlov, Ivan 26
penis 58
physicians 9, 10–11, 71
physiology 6, 71
pituitary gland 30, 40–41, 59
placenta 61, 71
plasma 46, 47
platelets 46, 47
positron emission tomography (PET) 15, 67
pregnancy 15, 60–61, 71
puberty 63, 71
pulse 42
pupil 35

R

red blood cells 19, 46–47, 51
reflexes 26, 27
Renaissance 6, 10
reproduction 58–61
respiratory system 48–51
retina 34, 35
Roentgen, Wilhelm 14, 67

S

saliva 39, 52, 53
scanning electron micrograph (SEM) 13
senses 32–39
sex cells 58
sight, sense of 34–35
skeleton 6, 16–21, 63
skin 32–33
skull 8, 17, 38, 39, 63
sleep 31
smell, sense of 31, 38
Spallanzani, Lazzaro 50
sperm 12, 58, 59, 60, 71
spinal cord 16, 26, 27, 39, 71
spine 16, 17
stem cells 19, 64
Steno, Nicholas 22
stomach 54
surgery 11, 68, 71
sutures 63, 71

T

taste, sense of 38–39, 52
tears 34
teeth 52, 53
transmission electron micrograph (TEM) 13, 71
temperature 6, 32, 46
tendons 23, 24
testes 40, 58
thalamus 30
thinking 31
thymus gland 40, 41, 45
thyroid gland 40
tissues 7, 71
tongue 38, 39, 48, 52, 53
torso 62, 71
touch, sense of 32, 33
trachea 21, 48, 49, 50, 51, 67
transplants 65

U V

ultrasound scans 15, 61
umbilical cord 61, 71
urinary system 56–57
urine 56, 57, 71
uterus 58, 59, 60–61
vagina 59
valves, heart 42
veins 19, 42, 43, 44, 45, 66, 71
vertebrae 16, 17
Vesalius, Andreas 10, 58, 66
video pills 15
villi 7, 55
viruses 45, 71
vocal cords 48, 49

W X Y Z

waste disposal 54, 55, 56–57
Watson, James 62, 67
white blood cells 19, 41, 45, 46, 47
X-rays 14, 18, 67, 71

Swammerdam, Jan 25
sweat glands 32
synapses 27, 71
synovial joints 21
systems 7, 71

Acknowledgments

Dorling Kindersley would like to thank:
Rajeev Doshi at Medimation (pp.26–27, 28–29, 40–41, and 50–51) & Arran Lewis (pp.38–39) for illustrations; Hilary Bird for the index; David Ekholm- JAlbum, Sunita Gahir, Andrea Mills, Susan St Louis, Lisa Stock, & Bulent Yusuf for the clipart; Sue Nicholson & Edward Kinsey for the wallchart; Monica Byles for proofreading.

For this relaunch edition, the publisher would also like to thank: Camilla Hallinan for text editing, and Carron Brown for proofreading.

The publisher would like to thank the following for their kind permission to reproduce their photographs:

(Key: a-above; b-below/bottom; c-center; f-far; l-left; r-right; t-top)

akg-images: 9cl, 11tl; **Alamy Images:** Mary Evans Picture Library 9tl, 9tr, 10cl, 12c, 12tl, 18cla, 30cra, 33tl, 34bc, 36tl, 47cl, 56tr; Dennis Hallinan 66bc; INTERPHOTO Pressebildagentur 42br; The London Art Archive 55tr; PHOTOTAKE Inc. 7c, 26bl, 29ca, 60c; The Print Collector 12cb, 16tl, 44cr, 50tr, 56crb, 60cr; Michael Ventura 15tr; World History Archive 29tl; **The Art Archive:** Bodleian Library, Oxford / Ashmole 399 folio 34r, 10tl; Private Collection / Marc Charmet 14tr; **The Bridgeman Art Library:** Bibliothèque de la Faculté de Médecine, Paris / Archives Charmet 46cl; Bibliothèque Nationale, Paris 8cr; Private Collection / Photo Christie's Images 63br; **Corbis:** Bettmann 24tl, 26cl, 41c, 50cl, 67bc; Christophe Boisvieux 31crb; CDC/ PHIL 13tr; EPA / Geoff Caddick 69bl; Frank Lane Picture Agency / Ron Boardman 13crb; The Gallery Collection 31tl, 44clb; Hulton-Deutsch Collection 22tr, 27ca, 49bl; John Zich/zrImages 67br; Gianni Dagli Orti 32c; Reuters / David Gray 69c; Ariel Skelley 62tr; Visuals Unlimited 7cr, 18clb, 19tr; Zefa / Flynn Larsen 33br; **DK Images:** The British Museum, London 42tl; The British Museum, London / Peter Hayman 8–9b, 66cl; Combustion 46–47c, 71tl; Courtesy of Denoyer – Geppert Intl / Geoff Brightling 55bc; Donks Models / Geoff Dann 13c; Arran Lewis 38–39; Linden Artists 57br; Medi-Mation 40–41c, 50–51bc; Courtesy of the Museum of Natural History of the University of Florence, Zoology section 'La Specola' / Liberto Perugi 11cr, 37tc, 44tr; Old Operating Theatre Museum, London / Steve Gorton 2cb, 4tr, 10–11b, 11cl; Courtesy of The Science Museum, London/ Adrian Whicher 8cl; Courtesy of The Science Museum, London / Dave King 3tl, 12cl, 12cr, 66cr, 69cr; Courtesy of The Science Museum, London / John Lepine 67tl; Jules Selmes and Debi Treloar 35tc; **Getty Images:** AFP / Andre Durand 15tr; AFP / Damien Meyer 21br; Henry Guttmann 11tr; Hulton Archive 35br; The Image Bank / Johannes Kroemer 70bl; Nick Laham 53tr; Win McNamee 65tl; Michael Ochs Archives 48cb; Popperfoto 28clb; Science Faction / Rawlins – CMSP 64crb; Stone / Ron Boardman 13bc; Taxi / Emmanuel Faure 15bl; Time Life Pictures / Mansell 37br; Topical Press Agency 41cr; Visuals Unlimited / Michael Gabridge 71bl; Gunther von Hagens' BODY WORLDS, Institute for Plastination, Heidelberg, Germany, www.bodyworlds.com: 68b; Courtesy of The Health Museum, Houston: 69tl; **iStockphoto.com:** 8tl; Roberto A. Sanchez 16bl; Jaroslaw Wojcik 64bc; **The Kobal Collection:** Carolco 65bl; Gaumont 46bl; Warner Bros 63tr; **Library of Congress, Washington, D.C.:** Cornish & Baker 63cr; **Mary Evans Picture Library:** 40bl; **Courtesy of The Old Operating Theatre, Museum & Herb Garret, London:** 68tr; **PA Photos:** AP Photo / Brian Walker 65tr; **Photolibrary:** Imagestate / David South 65bc; **Photo Scala, Florence:** The Museum of Modern Art, New York 31cra; **Science Photo Library:** 14cl, 23c, 25tr, 36cla, 59tl; Juergen Berger 64tr; Biology Media 25ca; Dr Goran Bredberg 37cr; A. Barrington Brown 62cla; Scott Camazine, Sue Trainor 18tl; Chemical Design 71br; CNRI 38bl, 41bc, 49cl, 49fcl; Christian Darkin 65crb; Equinox Graphics 70cb; Eye of Science 55tl; Simon Fraser 15c; GCa 17br; Steve Gschmeissner 19br, 32tr, 51tl; Innerspace Imaging 50bl; ISM / Alain Pol 57cr; Christian Jegou Publiphoto Diffusion 6tl; Nancy Kedersha 30br; James King-Holmes 67cr; Patrick Landmann 64cl; Dr Najeeb Layyous 61tl; Astrid & Hanns-Frieder Michler 41cl; Prof. P. Motta / Dept. of Anatomy / University 'La Sapienza', Rome 39br, 54cl; MPI Biochemistry/ Volker Steger 65c; Dr Gopal Murti 62clb; NIBSC 71cr; Susumu Nishinaga 64–65 (Background), 66–67 (Background), 68–69 (Background), 70–71 (Background); Omikron 35cb; US National Library of Medicine 28tr; Wellcome Department of Cognitive Neurology 15cl; Zephyr 14bc; **Still Pictures:** The Medical File / Charles Brooks 15tl; Ed Reschke 21cb; **Wellcome Library, London:** 6bl, 16cla, 22tl, 23bc, 23tc, 36cb, 38cl, 66cla

© 2008, by SOMSO models, www.somso.com: 2tr, 3tr, 4cla, 4cra, 18cr, 19ca, 24c, 27br, 30bl, 31bc, 32br, 46bl, 53bc, 53bl, 56bl, 56br, 58br, 59br, 60b, 61bl.

All other images
© Dorling Kindersley
For further information see:
www.dkimages.com

SOMSO
MODELLE
SINCE 1876